INTIMATE ENEMIES

INTIMATE ENEMIES
Jews and Arabs in a Shared Land

Meron Benvenisti

UNIVERSITY OF CALIFORNIA PRESS

Berkeley   Los Angeles   London

The author is deeply indebted to the Rockefeller Foundation and the Ford Foundation for a decade of generous support.

University of California Press
Berkeley and Los Angeles, California

University of California Press, Ltd.
London, England

Library of Congress Cataloging-in-Publication Data

Benvenisti, Meron, 1934–
    [Meḥol ha-ḥaradot. English]
    Intimate enemies : Jews and Arabs in a shared land /
Meron Benvenisti.
        p.   cm.
    Rev. English version of: Meḥol ha-ḥaradot.
    Includes bibliographical references and index.
    ISBN 0-520-08567-1 (alk. paper)
    1. Jewish-Arab relations—1973–   2. Intifada, 1987–
3. Persian Gulf War—Israel.   4. Israel—Politics and
government.   5. Israel. Treaties, etc.   Munaẓẓamat al-
Taḥīr al-Filasṭīnīyah, 1993 Sept. 13.   I. Title.
    DS119.7.B385813   1995
    956.9405'4—dc20   95-1933
                                               CIP

Printed in the United States of America

9 8 7 6 5 4 3 2 1

The paper used in this publication meets the minimum
requirements of American National Standard for
Information Sciences—Permanence of Paper for Printed
Library Materials, ANSI Z39.48–1984.

An earlier version of this book, in Hebrew, entitled *Mekhol
ha'kharadot* (Fatal Embrace), was published in 1992 by Keter
Publishing, Jerusalem.

CONTENTS

FOREWORD:
JEREMIAH AND JONAH

By Thomas L. Friedman

Meron Benvenisti is the Middle East expert to whom Middle East experts go for advice. Believe me I know. As a reporter for the *New York Times* in the Middle East for nearly a decade, I learned the difference between the mirage and the oasis. Meron is an oasis of knowledge in the intellectual deserts of the Middle East—deserts where charlatans and ideologues, hucksters and holy men, regularly opine and divine, unencumbered by facts, history, or statistics.

Whenever I wanted to cut through this mirage to the real, solid bedrock of what was happening and why, I called Meron—confident that his take would be original, his data unassailable, and his conclusions delivered without regard to whom they might offend or support. He was a man of the earth, a geographer and historian by training, and his opinions were always rooted in the earth, in the facts on the ground. He always connected me with the true Middle East, that often irrational, tribal world where people only do the right thing for the wrong reasons.

I first got to know Meron when I was the *New York Times* bureau chief in Jerusalem from 1984 to 1988. The fate of the West Bank and Gaza Strip was being hotly debated at that time. The question of the day was this: Had years of Israeli settlement building in the occupied territories gone so far as to inextricably knit Israel, Gaza, and the West Bank together, or could one still speak of Israel giving back these areas one day, despite the degree to which they had been integrated into the economic and political life of the Jewish state?

One of the remarkable things about that debate, though, was that for all its centrality in Israeli political life and for all of the attention it got in the international media, very little hard data had been assembled to inform the arguments of either side. Wishful thinking was the currency of this debate.

That was what led me to Meron's door. Working out of a small apartment, with a computer and a few researchers, he combed through Israeli government budgets, official abstracts, agricultural and water data, and brought them all together in something called "The West Bank Data Project," which painted a statistical picture of developments in the occupied territories. On a per capita basis (number of times quoted divided by the number of researchers involved), the West Bank Data Project, founded in 1982, was without question the most influential think tank in the debate about the occupied territories. Meron's conclusions alternately drove each side in that debate crazy and provided them with the statistical resources for their best arguments.

So, for instance, the settlers used to love to quote Meron's statistics about how deeply their rising numbers had sunk roots into the territories and how impossible it would be to expel them. But it drove them crazy when Meron showed how much it was costing the Israeli taxpayer to bus settler schoolchildren from their caravan homes on some remote hillock in the West Bank all the way to Jerusalem, where they could attend Jewish classes. The Palestinians hailed the West Bank Data Project for cataloguing just how much private and state land previously under Arab control had been expropriated by Israel since 1967. But it drove them crazy when Meron warned them that their maximalist approach to diplomacy and refusal to take half a loaf in order to slow Israeli settlement activity were tantamount to national suicide. While the peace talks remained deadlocked, he argued, the relentless worker bees of the Israeli settlement movement were throwing up prefab home after prefab home, making it harder and harder ever to separate Bethlehem from Jerusalem, or Tulkaram from Tel Aviv.

Meron was probably the most oft-quoted and oft-damned analyst in Israel in my day—Jeremiah and Jonah wrapped into one.

As time went by, though, Meron tired of being the reality principle for a debate in which no one was really interested in reality. So, much to the chagrin of journalists such as myself, he gave up the West Bank Data Project and began a life as a writer. Now, instead of providing the data for others to write about the territories from one political perspective or another, he deploys his own data in service of his own unique perspective. This book is one of the results. Meron's perspective is informed by his training at Harvard University as a political scientist, nurtured by his tenure as deputy mayor of Jerusalem from 1973 to 1978, and inflamed by his passion for the people, the stones, and the history of the land of Israel.

For years I had been after Meron to write just such a book as *Intimate Enemies*. Indeed, his stubborn refusal to do so really annoyed me. He was like this brilliant doctor whose clear-sighted ability to diagnose the heart of the problem, without even an x-ray machine, left you speechless. And when you asked for a prescription, this brilliant doctor said he did not do prescriptions. "But, doctor," you said, "the patient is ill, quacks are dispensing advice from soapboxes on every corner. Don't leave him like this." But he would just shake his head. He did not do prescriptions.

Well, with this book, the doctor is finally in, and I am glad he is. To understand this book, the reader must understand that Meron is what I would call a "tribal realist." That is, his view of the world, and the Arab-Israeli conflict, is essentially that humans are tribal beings and that tribal bonds, passions, memories, symbols, allegiances, and connections to pieces of land are the DNA building blocks, the double helix, at the core of Arab and Israeli behavior.

What Meron does in this book is take two very primordial tribal encounters between Israelis and Palestinians—the massacre of Palestinians by Israeli police on the Temple Mount in October 1990 and the handshake between intimate enemies Yasser Arafat and Yitzhak Rabin at the White House three years later—and posit them as the competing models for the future of this conflict. It is either the raised fist or the outstretched hand. There is not much in between. While Meron does not write out an explicit prescription for avoiding the former in favor of the latter, one can be gleaned from his analysis.

Meron acknowledges that as a tribal realist he was taken a bit by surprise by the Arafat-Rabin handshake. Being a man so rooted in the land of Israel and so sensitive to others' connections to the land and its symbols, he never believed that Arafat would surrender or that Rabin would accept that surrender and then live with a defanged PLO. What Meron missed in the past (which he acknowledges in this book) were some of the large historical forces that reshaped Israeli and Palestinian attitudes, despite their tribalism—forces such as the collapse of the Soviet Union and the Gulf War, which deprived Arafat of his economic lifeline. For Israelis, it was exhaustion with this conflict produced by the combination of the Palestinian uprising and the rising Israeli standard of living. This last factor—a growing desire among Israelis to separate themselves from the Palestinians so that Israeli society could live the good life without them—was critical in shaping an Israeli majority in favor of The Handshake.

In other words, it was the nightmare of extinction for Arafat and it was the dream of separation for Israelis that combined to produce this breakthrough. But Meron insists that while he may have missed some of the forces producing that embrace at the White House, the tribal elements have not gone away; they have been temporarily muted. And he is right. The dream of separation is possible in Gaza, a neatly self-contained unit. But how will it be fulfilled in Jerusalem and the West Bank, where the Jewish and Arab populations are so much more intertwined, and the symbolism of every stone is so much more potent? And if there is to be lasting separation, can it be based on Palestinian surrender? No, he essentially argues, it cannot, for there must be an element of equality in any final Israeli-Palestinian deal; otherwise a separation is no more sustainable than a divorce without an equitable division of property. The short-changed spouse will always be resentful and will come back to the judge for more.

And that gets back to the choice between the Temple Mount and the White House lawn. The Temple Mount represents the rage that is produced by a separation based on inequality; the White House lawn represents the hope inspired by separation based on equality.

So Meron leaves us with these three options: Will it be a continuation of the shepherds' war between peoples fated to share the same sidewalks, but who want it all. Or will it be the shepherds' pie, divided, slice by slice, not in equal shares but in shares based on the power relationship between the parties—meaning that the Jews will get the lion's portion, the Palestinians the beggar's bowl. Or will it be some third option—the Benvenisti option—call it shepherd's stew, in which Israelis and Palestinians somehow learn to share equally the territory of historic Palestine west of the river Jordan.

Meron describes this dream as one in which Jewish and Palestinian "cultural relations, human interactions, intimate coexistence and the attachment to a common homeland will be stronger than militant tribalism and segregation in national ghettos." Those who dream of such coexistence, Meron adds, "are entitled to suggest a system that combines ethnic and cultural separation within a common geopolitical framework."

That is not a prescription likely to win many adherents on either side for the moment; I have doubts about it myself. But even if you don't agree with Meron's conclusions, his analysis will provoke you to rethink the future of the conflict. As for me, I am just happy that the handshake at the White House has taken a professional pessimist, a tribal realist, and restored in him the power to dream the dream.

Thomas L. Friedman is Foreign Affairs columnist for the New York Times *and author of* From Beirut to Jerusalem.

CHAPTER ONE

CITY OF STRIFE

O nly rarely does history so dramatically summon together the three elements of classical tragedy: time, place, and action. Time—The morning of Monday, October 8, 1990, two months short of the third anniversary of the outbreak of the Palestinian uprising and two months after the start of the Persian Gulf crisis. Place—God's mountain, the Temple Mount and Holy of Holies, the sublime Haram, the holy compound near al-Aqsa, the uttermost mosque. Action—a bloody brawl between the children of Israel and the children of Ishmael, violent confrontation between the young men of two tribes, encapsulating a century of struggle. Seventeen people, all Arabs, were killed in the clash, and two hundred were wounded, among them fifteen Jews. As in every great tragedy, compressed within a few hours were all the struggle's contradictions, antagonisms, sensitivities, hatreds, apologetics, and primal urges. Although ceremonies of peace and reconciliation were soon to shroud the tribal hatreds in a shining fabric of words, documents, and agreements, the old animosities and primal urges would resurge, threatening to drown mounting hopes of peace in a sea of blood.

As in every true tragedy, people acted in accordance with an internal logic that imposed actions on them as if by fate. As with every great historic event, it is impossible to piece together what happened in a way that all those involved will endorse; each side has a persuasive version, containing its own amalgamation of cause and effect, and only its rendering will be commemorated in the pages of its own partisan history. As in every great historic event, too, there was that flash of light that illuminates the disturbing contours of the broader fabric. As in every great tragedy, too, the fundamental issue of survival shone brightly through the screen of evasions, ideology, and empty polemics that people attempted to stretch between them and their fears. People dared express their fears and hopes only through apocalyptic emotions and old myths. On October 12, 1990, the front page of the newspaper *A-Sha'ab* reported: "Palestinians who have in recent days returned from Saudi Arabia say that *ababil* birds are once again flying over the Holy Mosque in Mecca. . . . Simultaneously, the doves, descendants of those doves that were there during the days of the Prophet, have left Mecca and flown to Jordan. Palestinians who have come from there have said that the doves of Mecca have been seen in Ma'an and in Madaba [towns in Jordan]."

"I don't believe that story," a Palestinian teacher told the Israeli journalist Yehuda Litani, "but many people believe it. All those things come together into one picture, according to which Allah is preparing a great blow against all unbelievers, above all the Americans and Israelis." The almost mystical atmosphere that prevailed during the Intifada had metamorphosed, in the days before the incident, into a truly apocalyptic climate—not perhaps that of the world's end but nonetheless one of portentous events, things greater than man: "Just as God sent the *ababil* [black birds with owls' beaks] to save Mecca from the unbelievers, so Allah will save the Muslims," the teacher added. "A rumor has run through the city that Gershon Solomon's men [Jewish fanatics] plan to lay the cornerstone of the Third Temple within the al-Aqsa compound. There were preparations throughout the night. Our young people came in masses, ready for a real battle. They heard from religious leaders that it is a holy injunction to protect the third most holy mosque in Islam. They told us that the other two mosques, of Mecca and Medina, were under American occupation, and that we could not allow the Jews to take the last unconquered mosque."

On the other side, no less caught up in a mystical frenzy, were those who sought to do exactly what the Arabs sought to prevent. At his earlier trial for, among other things, planning to blow up the Dome of the Rock, Yehuda Etzion had declared: "I indeed believed it necessary for me to prepare an operation that I would call an operation to cleanse the Temple Mount of the building standing on its peak, on the site of the Holy of Holies . . . a building that has become a symbol and banner of the Islamic hold on the Temple Mount, and through it, on the entire country. . . . Not only must the Temple Mount be under our control as the focal point of our sovereignty over this land, but it is also forbidden for gentiles to set foot on it—in its central area—and all the more so for them to rule it." The Western Wall, Etzion added, "is the outer shell of the Temple Mount . . . and the possession of the Mount, as befits it, radiates its holiness and power over the entire land and the entire nation."

Ever since 1968 there have been extreme Jewish groups trying to upset the status quo on the Temple Mount. Some were arrested while preparing to blow up the mosques; others harassed the Muslim authorities, gave speeches in the Knesset defending the actions of the "Temple Mount Faithful," and handed out photomontages showing the Temple on a mosqueless mount. Yeshivot—Jewish religious seminaries—and other bodies publicly engaged in the preparation of ritual objects for use in the Temple. On the eve of the incident, the Temple Mount Faithful announced that they intended to stage a festive ceremony at which they would lay the cornerstone of the Third Temple.

"I don't believe that story," any sane Jew could recite in echo of his Palestinian counterpart, "but a lot of people believe it"— Jews and, mostly, Arabs. A few days before the Temple Mount incident, the authorities began handing out chemical warfare safety kits to the country's citizens. Fears of physical extermination, of a new Holocaust, fears that always gnaw away at the Jewish psyche, began to surface. Naturally, fear and the need to attribute events to supernatural powers were even stronger among the Palestinians. They have not done well in this world; naked reality has beaten them down mercilessly. They had all enlisted in a heroic effort to transform the reality of the Israeli occupation. They had bled, buried hundreds of their brave youths, and it had come to nothing. They had not been able to throw off the yoke of their Jewish taskmasters.

The sense of failure, the humiliation, the sorrow, and their powerlessness against forces stronger than they led the Palestinians to take refuge in faith in a superhuman savior. Attempts to explain reality in terms of an imminent redeemer and to see in their suffering the agony that heralds a magnificent future had never been foreign to them. The concept that the present is nothing but a dark antechamber leading to a shining future—the rebirth of the glorious Islamic past—is a pillar of Arab culture. Personal and collective fate coalesce in the figure of the *shaheed*, the person who gives his life for Allah. The shaheed does not die—he lives with God, as it is written: "Count not those who have been killed in the way of Allah as dead, nay, alive with their Lord, provided for, delighting in what Allah gave them" (Qur'an, sura Al-Imran 169). Death is not terrible, because it leads man to paradise, where he will win all the pleasures he did not know in this world. Neither are failure and defeat horrible, since they are but metaphors. Faith and rhetoric make every defeat a victory and every martyr a victorious hero. The sublime Haram is "the last remaining mosque." The battle for it will determine whether Palestine is lost or saved.

The Palestinians have always believed that the goal of Zionism is, as its name implies, control of the Temple Mount and the construction of the Third Temple. "The weeping of the Jews by the Wailing [Western] Wall and their kisses do not come of their love for the wall itself, but from their secret desire to win control of the Haram a-Sharif, as everyone knows," an Arab newspaper editorial declared in 1925. The Temple Mount and the Western Wall were the focus of the nationalist agitation and political struggle led by Haj Amin al-Husseini, the Grand Mufti of Jerusalem, who led his people to defeat. Now that the Jews had gained control of its entire area, young Palestinians had enlisted to defend their last outpost. In doing so, they were not only fighting the war for Palestine, but also joining the eternal struggle of believers against unbelievers on holy Arab land, under the command of the modern Saladin, Saddam Hussein.

This emotional time bomb did not occupy the thoughts of those who were to encounter it directly. From the end of the 1980s onward, the members of the Israeli security forces were the only Jews who had unmediated contact with the Arabs. Gone were the days of sympathetic middlemen who expressed understanding of, even empathy with, Palestinian frustration, who knew how to decipher the Arabs' cultural codes and convey them to the Jews. Twenty years before the Temple Mount incident, when al-Aqsa went up in flames, several Jews had stood in the company of Arab leaders and wept with them at the sight of fire destroying a Muslim holy place. Military personnel were removed from the Mount, and young Muslims circled the compound, carrying charred remnants, throwing stones, and shouting for revenge. No one tried to end the "agitation." In the end, Arab leaders asked that the Mount be sealed off, and that a temporary curfew be imposed; "Otherwise we won't be able to control the mob," they explained.

In October 1990, it was police officers who conducted the contacts with the Arab leaders. Being responsible for law enforcement, they expressed themselves in terms like "law and order" and "public safety." In the law, and especially the "Ordinance for the Prevention of Terrorism," the Arabs' expressions of frustration were defined as "agitation" and a direct threat to the existing regime. They were to be extirpated with all available force. The police were not looking for a violent confrontation. On the contrary, the rule they acted by was "a display of force is better than the use of force." Displaying force included, unavoidably, the humiliation of Arabs during searches, restrictions on movement, and the massive presence of armed policemen. It also required warnings like: "If a single small stone is thrown at us, we will fire live ammunition." But police officers also tried to dispel fears. They knew that the Arabs were organizing to thwart the plan of the Temple Mount Faithful to lay the Third Temple's cornerstone, and feared a violent clash. So they forbade Jews to demonstrate on the Mount and were pleased when the Supreme Court rejected the Faithful's suit to allow them access to the holy site.

The activity of Jewish provocateurs was considered "within the bounds of the law," a legitimate expression of pluralism in a democratic society. The police thus allowed the Faithful to demonstrate near the Temple Mount—but not on the Mount itself—and stood guard over them. The police took care to inform Arab leaders of the ban on the Temple Mount demonstration, hoping that the rejection of the Faithful's challenge by the High Court of Justice, the country's highest constitutional authority, would mollify the Palestinians. The level of the dialogue between the police and the Muslim leaders is epitomized in a segment of testimony from the officer responsible for the Temple Mount: "I spoke with the Mufti there . . . in a completely friendly way, we spoke with the Little Mufti and the Red Mufti, that's what we call them. I hope I'm not offending anyone. We really spoke in a friendly way, and the Red Mufti (I don't know his name, actually) told me: If Gershon Solomon comes up to the Mount there'll be a lot of blood and death here. I went to the Mufti and I told him, *dir balkum*, watch your step, you're making trouble. I don't like that. If a disturbance starts here, if they throw one stone over the Western Wall, we'll use gas, we'll shoot at you with gas." The police officer in charge thus did not even know the names of the spiritual leaders of a million Palestinians.

The Arabs accord the Jewish regime no legitimacy and see all its branches—judicial, legislative, and executive—as instruments of oppression and control directed against them. People who deny a government's legitimacy do not seek justice from it and have no faith in agents of the law. The "Little Mufti" and the "Red Mufti" therefore reacted with skepticism and disdain to the attempts of the police to reassure them. But the forces responsible for public safety could neither allow this nor understand it. From their point of view, the authority of law-enforcement agents is not open to challenge, and everyone must obey them. Anyone who dares rebel against their authority and that of the government that appointed them is no more than a common criminal, or, worse, a terrorist. People like that are to be treated in accordance with the Emergency Regulations, which are meant to foil all threats to the regime by means unamenable to normal law-enforcement procedures.

Israel's legal representatives were not only unaware of the deep feelings that pulsed through the Arabs that bitter morning, but also demanded loyalty and obedience, things the Arabs were unable to grant them. In the Arabs' eyes, the situation resembled the start of a boxing match in which one of the contestants also served as referee. For their part, the Jews saw a police patrol in a danger zone applying the principle that "a show of force is better than the use of force," rather than the principle of dialogue, to specific lawbreakers.

As with every great historic event, opinions were divided as to the causes of the first outbreak of violence. Yet from the moment the first bullet was fired, or from the moment the first stone was thrown, the incident took on the cast of a real battle. True, the battle was unequal: on one side were unarmed men fighting with stones, sticks, and iron bars; on the other were regular detachments with firearms, troops that at short notice could call down the full power of a sovereign state. But during the critical moments, the Arabs' numerical superiority compensated for their limited weaponry: they won the first act of the engagement. One of the policemen recounted: "And there we were alone, 45 men facing 3,000. . . . it's terrifying . . . to face the *shabab* [Arab youth], thousands throwing rocks and iron pipes at you. . . . They come closer and closer, and the whole time they never stop throwing all those things at you . . . and you see such great fervor in their eyes, as if they were in the midst of prayer or something. . . . Here, yesterday we had to retreat from the Temple Mount to regroup and ask for reinforcements, and that's never happened to our men." An Arab youth put it this way: "When the policemen began to shoot, we began to throw stones at the police. Afterwards we charged them and drove them out of the Haram."

Both sides stripped themselves of their ideological and religious garb—the police abandoning their "law-enforcing" role—and launched into a primeval contest, a shepherds' war, in which the motivating force was hatred of the other, classic tribal strife in no need of subtle exegesis. The fact that on one side civilians fought with sticks and stones while on the other uniformed men wielded lethal weapons was of no importance to either. Each side saw itself facing an enemy that had to be eliminated. Each side identified the life-or-death element in the clash. It was neither an attempt to restore public order nor a defense of Islamic holy places. They entered our territory, and we ejected them. They humiliated us and drove us out in disgrace.

The curtain then rose on the second act of the tragedy. The Jews wished, at any price, to take revenge on the "mob" and recapture the holy mountain. They did this by exploiting their relative advantage—firearms. After the incident, there were explanations of and excuses for the savage counterattack of the uniformed forces. It was said that the supply of rubber and plastic bullets had run out; it was argued that the Arabs did not retreat despite gunshots in the air, that there were strategic points that had to be defended at any cost—the Western Wall, the police station on the Mount, and the policemen inside it—and that these were in danger. Critics said the police panicked.

Apparently all these explanations are correct. It would seem, however, that an uncontrollable motivating force was the primal need to deal a blow to the enemy and be rid of him, so restoring personal and collective pride. Seventeen Palestinians were killed by Israeli bullets. The police sprayed automatic fire indiscriminately into the crowd, running down those who fled, and not giving quarter until they fell in pools of their own blood. The minutes of the judicial inquiry record:

QUESTION: What did he do, the "minority person"? [In Israeli legalese, non-Jews are "minority persons."] Did he try to flee? Did he throw stones?

ANSWER: He tried to flee, he was kind of in shock and tried to flee. He didn't know.

QUESTION: Why was it necessary to shoot him?

ANSWER: . . . I don't know . . . when I turned around he, the policeman, was talking to him.

QUESTION: Spoke with the minority person? Before the gunfire? And then he shot him?

ANSWER: Yes.

Mohammed Shaloud told the magistrate: "They told us to kneel down on the floor and we put our hands on the backs of our necks. After that they began shooting us." A policeman vaguely confirmed the Arab version.

QUESTION: Is there evidence that they shot and even killed people from the group of worshipers?

ANSWER: To say whether they killed any? I don't know. There were gunshots.

QUESTION: There were gunshots on that group?

ANSWER: There were shots in the direction of the group.

Gratuitous cruelty? Those who judge the security forces' actions according to the criteria of "public order" will condemn them for what they did, since the circumstances did not require the use of firearms. But the policemen considered themselves to be in battle. During one of the inquiries, a policeman referred to the detainees as "prisoners of war." The magistrate rebuked him and emphasized that they were not at war. One of those present summed it up: "It seems as if the Border Guard policemen thought that they really were at war, or at least that is how they behaved on the Mount."

The gunshots were not aimed at human beings, at individuals, but rather at a large and threatening horde, devoid of human features. Dehumanization is a precondition of shooting at the enemy. In war, soldiers shoot to kill and get medals for it. Yet a man does not have to be at the front to feel that he is at war. When he feels that his primary national and cultural values hang in the balance, and that he is ready to fight with all his strength to defend them, or when such a feeling is instilled into him, he feels he is at war. This is true whether he is dressed in civilian clothing or in the uniform of a police patrolman.

This was how the Palestinians felt: "A man with his face covered came within five meters of a Border Guard policeman with a block in his hands. The policeman fired into the air. The boy was not deterred, and then he was shot." "Our boys do not consider the facts. Everything was in an atmosphere that was about to explode, before a huge victory by Allah, and they felt they were Allah's soldiers," an Arab journalist said, adding, "Yesterday, when Dibhi reached . . . the Temple Mount, he told those around him that he wanted to become a shaheed. He had a feeling that he was going to be killed. He told everyone that he was not frightened. And he really was killed. . . . the children are fighters, they sacrifice their lives for the homeland, for Allah."

The willingness to sacrifice one's life on the altar of nation and religion is a consequence of despair—despair at the chances of being freed from the occupation by other means—and also a reaction to humiliation, the constant wounding of Arab pride: "Your soldiers and policemen treat us with horrible crudity—blows, slaps, kicks, torture during interrogation." An Israeli journalist wrote: "A boy (a policeman) stood there with a lit cigarette, which he waved in the faces of dignitaries, shouting at them, '*Ruhu*, get out of here.' He didn't understand Arabic; he only heard the tone of anger, and it irritated him. 'This is our place,' one of the members of the council shouted. '*Allah hua akbar—* Allah is supreme!' The finger was already on the trigger. A firecracker was thrown under the Mufti's feet. . . . 'This is our place!' a lame elder leaning on a cane screamed hysterically. The Border

Guard officer did not hesitate for a second—he grabbed him by the collar, pushed him forward, and sent him rolling over the stones. . . . The humiliation—it's a wonder that they still don't understand it—hurts much more than physical violence."

The abandoned battleground was covered with bloodstains and empty cartridges, and there were pockmarks on the marble walls of the mosques. "I've never seen so much blood in one place," a witness said. "On the floor, on the big flagstones, and on the large gates leading to the hall of the al-Aqsa mosque; there was a lot of blood on the main gate . . . and from there a trail of blood all the way to the steps leading to the Dome of the Rock . . . blood-covered hands left imprints on the walls and doors . . . and a great desire for revenge remained; . . . now they are preparing what they call a reprisal for the Temple Mount . . . revenge, revenge, that's the word you hear everywhere." After each of the murders committed thereafter—the slaughter of Jewish women and the stabbing of passersby—the murderers declared that they were avenging their brothers' blood spilt on the holy site.

The silence that descends after a battle permeated the Temple Mount. Shock, outrage, and grief spread quickly through the passageways of the Old City, and from there to Jerusalem's neighborhoods. Soon, snowballing all the while, they reached the refugee camps in Gaza, Hebron, and Nablus. The wildest demonstrations occurred, unexpectedly, in the Galilee—in Nazareth, and in Tamra, the hometown of one of the dead men, an Israeli Arab. Had the Israelis used the methods standard at that time, dozens would have died. But the stunned Israelis held their fire. They were in shock, too, and needed time to recover. While there were many victims among the Arabs and their rebellion had been suppressed, the sacrifice had not been in vain—

they had succeeded in stripping the Israelis of their mantle of "preservers of public order" and in presenting them to the world (and, most of all, to the Israelis themselves) unadorned—as a dominating ethnic group with a monopoly on legal violence, which it used indiscriminately against a dominated and defenseless ethnic group.

Of course, this was not the first time that the bias of the Israeli law-enforcement system had been bared in public. The years of the Intifada had eliminated what was left of the myth of a "benign" occupation watching over the safety and prosperity of a "protected population" in accordance with international law. The Temple Mount incident, in the heart of "united Jerusalem," under the rule and law of a democratic, liberal Western state, forced Israelis to look long and hard at naked reality. The trauma was serious. They were reacting, not to the number of Arab victims, but rather to the damage to their self-image and their reputation in the world, to which they now seemed a disoriented, cruel regime. As such, their reaction to the trauma was not a painful confrontation with reality but an almost desperate attempt to reconstruct their web of evasions and excuses and, most of all, to believe in it again. This attempt began with a theory of geopolitical conspiracy—Saddam Hussein and his ally, Yassir Arafat, had plotted the disturbances in order to raise the Muslim world against the United States and its Zionist puppet.

The attempt to fit the incident into an international context and to deny its local, intercommunal character was spurious even in the eyes of those government ministers who floated the conspiracy theory. As a result, the Israelis soon began to make arguments that were mirror images of the Arab claims. In the Israeli version, there was no provocative attempt to take control of the

Temple Mount and cause damage to Islamic holy places. On the contrary, there had been an organized Arab attack on defenseless Jewish worshipers at the Western Wall. Forty-eight hours after the incident, an Israeli judge could state categorically: "At 10:30 A.M. blocks and stones began hurtling down on worshipers in the Western Wall compound. . . . It took the police a certain amount of time to organize themselves . . . and halt the stone-throwing into the Western Wall compound. When the policemen found this unsuccessful, they used their weapons, at first rubber bullets and, in the end, live ammunition. . . . The attack turned the Sukkot holiday—the holiday of joy—into a holiday of sorrow and grief. The Western Wall compound is eternally holy, and it is clear that whoever plans and carries out a mass attack on this holy place on a holy day cannot afterwards expect that the attack will be ignored."

The police had done their job, intervening to prevent danger to human (Jewish) life, which could not have been done without the use of firearms. "The result of the use of firearms was most tragic, but necessary under the circumstances, given the mass disturbances," the judge found. The charge that Jewish provocation had roused the Arabs' reaction "seems totally unfounded and there is no doubt that the rioters and their leaders, who incited and organized them, are responsible for this grave event." The claim that "the Arabs started it" was given the official stamp of approval by an investigatory commission, the Zamir Committee, which determined that "the incident began to snowball when menacing and violent calls were suddenly made over the loud-speakers, and immediately thereafter huge quantities of stones, building materials, and metal were rained down on Israeli policemen."

The question of who started it—or, in other words, what the reason was and who was guilty—was more controversial than the incident itself. Context is a matter of ethnic affiliation. The attribution of cause and effect is not a matter of objective-logical derivation but rather of one-sided conceptions. The chain of intercommunal violence is nourished by opposing definitions of the relationship between challenge and response. What one group sees as a challenge looks like a response to another. It almost seems as if it were possible to order causes and effects into a chain agreed upon by both sides, the chain of violence would break. As in a children's fight, however, the shout "he started it" is a battle cry.

The inequality of forces that caused the loss of life to be restricted to the Arab side; the exposure to the world of the specious presumption on the part of the Israelis that they were the protectors of "public order"; and well-grounded testimony that confuted Israeli attempts at obfuscation—all these created profound political distress. As usual, the Israelis blamed their plight on ineffective public relations. Searing international criticism and the threat of sanctions against Israel gradually silenced the internal debate. The instinctive tribal reflex—banding together against the hostile outside world—functioned as usual. The main response, however, was not evasion and self-justification, but rather psychological repression and amnesia. Only a few days later, the memory of the incident had dissipated, and it was seen as but another instance of Intifada violence. The mechanism that consecrates confrontations and fixes them in the calendar of Israeli memory did not work this time. There were no Jewish casualties, so there were no ceremonies on the seventh and thirtieth days, and no monuments were erected. Most of all, there were no calls for "an appropriate response."

Grief and the Arab desire for revenge did not occupy the Israelis, who were caught up in the incident's implications for their self-image. A government commission of inquiry, judicial investigations, and political discussions focused on the operational, political, and moral aspects. The pointed criticism on the one hand and apologetics on the other turned, as usual, into a mutual goring by left and right. The ethnocentric viewpoint internalized the incident and made it into a test of the Jewish value system. Had the police soiled the "purity of arms" with their brutality? Had shortcomings been discovered in the law-enforcement system and governmental oversight? Had there been negligence at the political level in controlling the security services? In short, was it a blot on Jewish honor, as the Jews themselves conceived it?

This ideological and moral distress, and the strident debates it brought on, revealed a sensitivity to liberal-moral values, but also helped suppress the incident's tragic side—the loss of human life, the personal and collective grief and the desire for revenge on the part of the members of a different community. Their sensibilities dulled to the sacrifice made by the enemy—another aspect of the process of dehumanization characteristic of a wartime atmosphere—the Jews refused to grasp the context when a wave of murders began, with Arab killers lunging at their victims with cries of "Allah hua akbar."

Israelis felt that any understanding of the circumstantial connection or the motive for such murders was tantamount to excusing the crime. To understand the Arab desire to avenge a deed that had shocked and shamed Jews as well as Arabs was to sympathize with the murderers' motives. The murder of women, children, and other innocent civilians had to be seen as without antecedent, even if it took place a short while after the incident on the Temple Mount.

On the morning of Sunday, October 21, 1990, three weeks after the incident on the Temple Mount, a nineteen-year-old Arab laborer stabbed three people to death and wounded a small boy in the Baka neighborhood of Jerusalem. One of the victims, a policeman, Charlie Shloush, hesitating to shoot to kill, grappled with the murderer, and was slain. The young Arab ran amok, stabbing four people in less than twenty minutes on three different streets before being caught, beaten, and arrested.

The Jewish public's trauma was so great that there were almost no attempts at retribution against Arabs, as had been the case after previous murders. The sense of grief and terror were especially acute because the murder had taken place in a tranquil Jewish neighborhood whose residents had no direct connection, either personal or indirect, with the violent conflict. Especially appalled were those in the neighborhood who belonged to left-wing groups—in fact, most of the leaders of the Peace Now movement lived in Baka.

The left fostered a worldview that externalized the conflict and focused it on the territories: there, beyond the psychological barrier of the Green Line, the Palestinians fought for their national liberation; there unbearable things happened. They themselves lived in metropolitan Israel: the territories were an occupied colony. Their obligation as liberals and freedom fighters was to oppose the "corrupting occupation," and to solve the conflict by "the establishment of a Palestinian state beside Israel."

Defining the conflict in geopolitical terms allowed them to evade its endemic intercommunal nature.

The Temple Mount incident shattered this worldview. Even the members of Peace Now realized that no geopolitical solution could prevent contention between Jewish worshipers below, in the Western Wall compound, and Arab worshipers above, on the Temple Mount—with only the Western Wall itself separating them. For this reason they chose to phrase their position on the Temple Mount incident in terms of "the brutal use of force" and "the security forces' uncontrolled behavior" rather than in terms of "down with the occupation."

The murders in Baka literally brought the conflict to the doorsteps of the left. It had erupted within their daily routine, in which there was time allotted to working against the occupation, to meetings with Palestinians, and to chamber-music concerts. One of the murders took place adjacent to the doorway of a house where, a few hours earlier, there had been just such a concert, attended by many members of Peace Now. One Arab was also there. He described his feelings thus: "In the middle of the program I asked myself where I was. A few kilometers from my house in Ramallah, but really thousands of miles away. . . . after the concert, when I went home, I thought to myself that I had discovered the secret of the Jewish people. They have nerves of iron. They are able to suspend the ugliness of daily life and turn into consumers of culture. That's how they survive. I returned to my neighborhood thinking that we were not like that. We live the Intifada twenty-four hours a day. Live and think and eat and drink only Intifada. . . . But now I had heard what was going on in Baka, that seemingly quiet neighborhood . . . and I said to myself that I had apparently been party to a singular moment that might not be repeated. . . . If it had happened there, no corner of the country was safe any longer. . . . And the thought came to me . . . that if we were responsible, then we would have to get up and leave this beloved land, with all the sorrow involved, to your and our madmen, for them to fight and kill and spill blood, but without us. Who knows? Maybe for a few years and maybe forever."

This Arab expressed the duality of place and emotion well. He lives, thinks, eats, and drinks "only Intifada" "twenty-four hours a day" because the Jews, with their big, strong army, have displaced the violence to his home ground. Only he and members of his community fear what the night may bring. His hosts, with their "iron nerves," are able "to suspend the ugliness of daily life" because their daily lives are simply not ugly. As members of the dominant community, they are shielded from the violent reality of the conflict and able to conduct normal lives. The "ugliness" creates a controlled shock in them, causes them to demonstrate a bit, write a bit, but never to experience the totality of the conflict.

Their "iron nerves" did not function, however, when the "ugliness" reached Jewish liberal thresholds. Heedless of geographical boundaries, the conflict now knocked ominously at the door. Translated from the sterile and theoretical language of "two states for two peoples" into the language of fear, it forced everyone to eye everyone else suspiciously—is he friend or foe? It was suddenly impossible to identify with the oppressed Arab—instead, the instinctive reaction was one of recoil. The world was divided according to tribal affiliation, and all Jews were brothers.

But the murder in Baka brought another shock. The breach separating Jew from Arab had already widened into an abyss.

Now a destructive force attacked the rough stitches tying together Jewish society, and began to unravel them. The anger of the neighborhood's old-timers—the disadvantaged, mostly Asian and North African Jews who had come to the neighborhood in the 1950s from transit camps—was directed against the "lefties," the intellectuals of the upper middle class, the Arab-loving bleeding hearts. "Death to the traitors!" echoed through Baka along with "Death to the Arabs!" A leaflet distributed in the neighborhood denounced Peace Now: "Who does Peace Now care about when the Jewish people grieves and mourns the murder of Jews? The Arabs!"

Leftists were attacked on the streets, and their homes were stoned. A member of the city council who had participated in demonstrations organized by Women in Black, a women's peace group, was told: "Idiot, because of you things like this happen. Idiot, slut, whore, liar . . . you trampled the flag of Israel . . . disgusting Israel-hater . . . dress in black for the rest of your life."

The peace activists had wanted to serve as a bridge to peace, but the Israeli mob felt like the Protestant extremist Rev. Ian Paisley in Belfast when he said: "A traitor and a bridge are very much alike: both go over to the other side." For them, those sensitive to human values betray tribal values. The leftists wished to feel that they shared a common fate with their neighbors, but they were rudely rejected. They refused to believe that their neighbors, with whom they lived "in harmony, pluralism, and tolerance, a melting pot of openness," had fostered such anger and hatred against them. They therefore put the blame on right-wing politicians and the followers of Rabbi Meir Kahane, who laced the neighborhood with poison. "The delicate balance so characteristic of Baka, between left and right, between liberals and nationalists, was violated by a sweep of a cruel blade, and by lawless and irresponsible words," said Haim Baram, a left-wing journalist. Anat Peri, a reader, corrected him, noting: "[It is a] common [illusion] in this neighborhood, as in other similar neighborhoods where luxurious houses stand next to wretched housing projects, that the neighborhood is integrated. . . . The dividing line between the two is clear and amazingly sharp, and if those standing on one side do not see it, those who stand on the other side see it all too well. [The rightist Knesset member] Geula Cohen did not provoke the division, hatred, and bitterness. She only used them for her own purposes."

The conflict traced impermeable boundaries between the Jewish and Arab communities, demanding communal loyalty of everyone: "Are you with us or with our foes?" Intellectual and political energy were directed at coping with the substantive and conceptual problems raised by what was perceived as a life-or-death struggle; the public agenda was determined by its constraints; and the left-right divide was defined according to attitudes to it. Social and cultural tensions among Israelis broke out under cover of confrontations between "peace activists" and "nationalists." Testifying to the inability of reality to influence petrified ideology, a Baka resident said: "What's really important is the recognition that this incident, as horrible as it was, reinforces people holding opposing opinions. Whoever was right-wing saw his beliefs reconfirmed, as did whoever was left-wing."

Amazingly, the operational conclusion drawn by right and left, based on diametrically opposing ideologies, was the same—keep the Arabs out. "Don't let the Arabs work here. Make them feel shitty. Let them work in Kuwait, in Jordan, but not get anywhere near us. The solution isn't the death penalty or life imprisonment. The solution is simply not to mix with them. We need a Jewish state with four walls and that's it," said a relative of the murdered policeman, Charlie Shloush.

"The goal is not to fall in love with them, but to disengage from them," said the Peace Now spokesman Amiram Goldblum, a Baka resident whose house was attacked by "right-wingers." He saw disengagement as the first stage on the way to establishing a Palestinian state. "What do I care about left or right?" asked a columnist who generally expressed the consensus. "Independent of my opinions on the proper or desirable future political solutions, the current situation is no longer tolerable. . . . We must create a buffer, restrict contact, separate us from them for the interim."

For some, "disentanglement" meant forbidding Arabs to enter Jewish areas; for others it was a "voluntary transfer." The main thing was to wake up one morning and realize that all the "others" had disappeared. Right and left were united in their feeling that radical surgery was necessary, regardless of controversies over political solutions. "It's a fact of life that tomorrow's crazy murderer might be the plasterer in the building across the street . . . the man coming down the street opposite me. I don't want that man in the street here, nor the delivery boy from the store." Murders that took place after the ones in Baka sharpened this feeling and made separation a central question on the public agenda, as the main tool used by the government to combat violence, and as a basis for future peace initiatives.

The chain of violence that had begun on the Temple Mount perpetuated itself. A few months after the murders in Baka, Arieh Shloush, a soldier brother of the slain policeman Charlie Shloush, sought revenge, opening fire on a car near Hebron and wounding its passengers. In military court he explained that he had known no rest since his brother's death, and that he had felt an uncontrollable urge to attack Arabs. In major Israeli cities, Jews were murdered by Muslim extremists who subsequently cited the Temple Mount incident as one of their motives. The cry "Allah hua akbar!" became a nightmare for Jews, and they heard it both when it was uttered and when it was not.

The city of peace had turned into a battleground. Violent acts were committed everywhere: in the alleys of the Old City and at bus stops in the heart of residential neighborhoods far from the old border, still optimistically called "the seam." The attacks were generally made with knives, and the motives were either personal, such as revenge for the killing of an Arab by the security forces, or religious fundamentalist. Testifying to the random character of the violence, a young woman from Ramallah told her interrogators that she decided to buy a knife and murder a Jewish policeman because she had a dream "and woke up in the morning with a headache."

From the outbreak of the Palestinian uprising in December 1987, the rebellion in Jerusalem was no different from that in Gaza and on the West Bank. Commercial strikes, stone throwing, attacks on passersby, car torchings, demonstrations, slogan painting, and the raising of Palestinian flags took place in Jerusalem with the same frequency and with the same potency as in the territories. On the face of it, this should not have been surprising. Jerusalem, the commercial, social, cultural, and political center of the West Bank, and the largest Arab city in Israel, the religious and national symbol of the Palestinians, has been the focus of the Palestinian resistance since 1968. After nineteen years of relative acquiescence, the Palestinians rebelled, regaining their lost self-esteem in the process and making the intercommunal strife between Jew and Arab—hitherto so successfully camouflaged by thick layers of public relations and abetted by Arab docility—a visible, undeniable reality.

Although Jerusalem's physical space was unified after the Six-Day War in 1967, the city's psychological space did not merge with it. Indeed, the absence of physical barriers reinforced the need for emotional ones. Segregation and alienation cut across all levels of communal interaction, from nursery to graveyard, and cannot be explained merely as a product of disagreements about the political future of Jerusalem. So basic is the cleavage that a decisive component of the self-identity of Jews and Arabs alike is not who they are, but who they are not.

Such polarization creates a breeding ground for intercommunal strife, a volatile environment that can be ignited by the smallest spark. The curious mixture of confrontation, segregation, and cooperation that had characterized Jerusalem for almost a generation was upset. The image of the Holy City cherished by millions, a peaceful and cosmopolitan unity of opposites, suffered a tremendous, perhaps mortal, blow. In its place, the true nature of the City of Peace emerged: harsh, exclusionary, intolerant; a collection of alienated islands—Jewish and Arab, religious and secular, oriental and occidental—separated by deep ravines, all smoldering under a dazzling, remorseless sun. But the Israelis have chosen to ignore this reality—they have chosen to see in the "united city" a place cut off from its natural hinterland, an inseparable part of Israel.

The pathetic attempt to suppress this reality was especially common among moderate Israelis. It was a way for them to give free reign to their patriotic emotions while nonetheless feeling that they were willing "to give up the rest of the territories." Psychological repression to balance contradictory values has occurred since the capture of the eastern part of the city and has been put to the test whenever violence has increased, or when there has been intercommunal contention against the background of unilateral action by Israeli governments. The Intifada robbed Israelis of whatever illusions about "peaceful coexistence" among the residents of Jerusalem remained to them. When the sham distinction between Jerusalem and the territories was erased, Israelis felt that they had been slapped in the face. The continuing acts of violence, and especially the recurring murders on the border between the Arab and Jewish neighborhoods, gave rise to spontaneous, instinctive, emotional feelings of dread, revulsion, hatred, desire for revenge, sadness, and grief. Arabs who chanced to be near the site of an attack were beaten and their automobiles stoned. Furious crowds stormed Arab neighborhoods, causing damage to homes and yards. Chants like "Death to the Arabs" echoed in their throats and were smeared on the walls.

The expressions of malevolence and the physical attacks quickly died down: many who had participated even repented of their outbursts. But spontaneity and authentic reactions did not come from the politicians, whose well-considered responses were meant to serve their factional goals and their ideology. Here was the incendiary of the extreme right who wished to exploit the hatred and bitterness for his own ends; here was the Greater Israel partisan for whom there is no difference between Tel Aviv, Jerusalem, and Nablus; here was the apostle of territorial compromise, for whom the attacks proved the necessity of relinquishing territories.

The gap between the public's feelings and the positions of the politicians was expressed in the dispute that broke out over the erection of a security fence that would divide a Jewish neighborhood from the Arab areas bordering on it. The need to wall in the anxiety physically, to define a psychological boundary behind which Israelis could feel secure, led to a stubborn demand to erect a protective wall that would prevent Arabs from entering Jewish neighborhoods. In a city through which tens of thousands of Arabs circulate in the course of their work, where they use the public transportation facilities, the demand bordered on the absurd.

Asked to give their opinion, the security authorities were not (as they usually are) of one mind, but many politicians felt that erecting a fence would contradict the principle of the "united city." The most adamant of these was Mayor Teddy Kollek; the originator and nurturer of the myth of the united city could not acquiesce in the destruction of his life's work, nor could he allow his prestige as the father of "coexistence" to be besmirched.

The iron fence, 350 yards long, was built nevertheless, a physical barrier dividing the antagonistic communities. Jerusalem thus joined the conflict-riven cities through the hearts of which a "peace line," a "green line," or just "the wall" stretches. This physical expression of the dissipation of a mirage was hard to bear. There was a typically emotional reaction to the evaporation of this illusion. Israelis had always had a paternalistic attitude to the Arabs, one that assumed that most of them had come to terms with the unification of the city and enjoyed its benefits. In this view, a small minority of dissenters existed, of course, but they were incited by outside forces.

This outlook was now abandoned in favor of seeing Arab dissenters as a community of agitators who pursued violence for its own sake. The change in attitude was not fundamental, since both perceptions deny that the Arab community has the capacity to act as an independent entity possessing self-consciousness and autonomous judgment, defining its own goals and acting to achieve them by means it has chosen. For many years, Israelis had lived the illusion of the "united city," but this illusion was able to survive only as long as they believed that they were the only legitimate collective, while the "others" were merely a hodgepodge of people lacking any independent identification and open to manipulation by the Jewish state through "tolerance" and material improvements.

The overused metaphor of the carrot and the stick best describes this approach. The image of the Arab community as a passive entity, together with a policy of paternalistic coexistence, allowed Israelis to ignore the coercive aspect of their rule, and thus evade the contradiction between their self-image as peace-loving liberals and the regime they had imposed on the "united city." The fact that an autonomous Arab community existed now hit them squarely between the eyes, but in "discovering" it, they chose to define it as "an illegitimate collective, a community of terrorists and disturbers of the public peace." Now there was no sense in perpetuating the concept of paternalistic coexistence and investing efforts in improving the Arabs' living conditions—there was no point in this unless the Israelis were the initiators and largesse was bestowed from above. Now it was possible to see any response to Arab demands as caving in to pressure, and as a manifestation of weakness. For this reason, the job of dealing with intercommunal relations was handed over to the security forces, which followed the principle of the "show of force or use of force" rather than pursuing dialogue.

With the security forces, there was no need to repress the coerciveness of the regime. On the contrary, the threat was seen as one of life or death, and the conflict as being over absolute values. In such a confrontation there was no escaping the exercise of force. Existential fears were sharpened by the Temple Mount incident and the violent chain reaction that followed it. Before that, Israelis could attribute violence in Jerusalem to "the problem of the territories" and look for political solutions; but now, with the confrontation focused in Jerusalem, even the purest Israeli peaceniks did not see the Temple Mount and the Western Wall as diplomatic negotiating chips.

The murders in Jewish neighborhoods in West Jerusalem had spread the conflict from areas where the Arab population was concentrated, across the "seam" that divided Arab and Jewish neighborhoods, into the heart of the Jewish sector, blurring the lines defining the intercommunal frontier. Fear of the knife-wielders grew, as did dread of endemic, insoluble violence. The illusory safety net—in the form of conventional political solutions and routine slogans—was torn. Faith in the government's ability to find a rational solution that would rescue Israel from the affliction of perpetual strife was challenged. Worst of all, the traditional political and ideological positions were blurred. People of the left and right found themselves preaching identical responses. Radical Israelis felt the need to return to the consensus, and those who had once boasted of their close ties with Arabs allowed themselves to express their antipathy in public. Jews refused to employ Arabs (even cleaning women were fired), and many Jews terminated personal and professional links with Arabs.

Methods of punishment and deterrence that had traditionally not been allowed in "united Jerusalem" were now applied in the city without there being any public or political repercussions—extended curfews were imposed on Arab neighborhoods; young Arabs were refused entry to the Temple Mount; residents of the territories were kept from entering Jerusalem, even in order to travel from the northern West Bank to its southern part; thousands of Arabs who made their livings in West Jerusalem were detained at roadblocks; Arabs who crossed the old Green Line, separating East Jerusalem from West Jerusalem, were sent home. All these steps completely eliminated the official distinction between the treatment of East Jerusalem and the treatment of the West Bank. East Jerusalem had become occupied territory, just like the cities and villages of the West Bank.

The elimination of this specious distinction between "united Jerusalem" and "the territories" could actually serve as an opening for an analysis of the system of governing Jerusalem during the first quarter-century since its liberation, and for examining the principles and concepts that guided it—principles and concepts that most Israelis consider to be consistent with universal and democratic values. The Israeli government imposed Israeli law, justice, and administration on Jerusalem, establishing permanent operating procedures that most Israelis consider nonnegotiable, except on marginal matters.

The annexation of Jerusalem to Israel in 1967 was accomplished unilaterally and without consulting the inhabitants of the annexed territory. The Israelis did not seek international legitimacy for their move because they knew that international law does not recognize unilateral annexation, and that the international community could not grant legitimacy to an illegal act. They were ready to endure dozens of censure resolutions—as long as they were not accompanied by sanctions. The Israelis

placed their faith in the force of habit and on the institutionalization of the status quo over time. In fact, over the years, the
world's condemnation has grown fainter, to the point where
when it is voiced anew—as, for instance, after the Temple Mount
incident—the Israelis have termed it "interference in internal
affairs." The Israelis were especially angry at the United States,
which dared define their control of Jerusalem as a "military occupation," or at least did not object to that definition.

The Israelis have not sought legitimation from the people
they annexed: they demanded compliance, not consent. Of
course, they declared that the pinnacle of their hopes was "Arab
recognition of Israeli rule," but they really hoped that the Arabs
would *not* concede the legitimacy of the Israeli regime. To ask it
of the Arabs would imply that they constituted a collective capable of granting such legitimation, which would mean ipso facto
that they were autonomous—in which case they would almost
certainly *deny* Israel's legitimacy and refuse to recognize it.

The Israelis therefore disavowed the right of the Palestinians
to disavow Israeli legitimacy, and trusted to the Palestinians
never to recognize Israel's regime. This made it simultaneously
possible to ignore the existence of a Palestinian collective, to
evade doubts about the legitimacy of the Israeli regime, to
believe that Israelis really did want Arab recognition, and to reap
the benefits of the Palestinian refusal to recognize Israeli control
of Jerusalem. This was how Israelis preserved the illusion that
they remained committed to universal democratic values.

Just to be sure, the government of Israel made sure that the
Palestinians would have no opportunity to express their nonrecognition in accepted political ways. Israel did not automatically grant Palestinians in East Jerusalem citizenship, as is normal

practice when territories are annexed—as, in fact, Israel itself did in 1948 with regard to the Israeli Arabs. The Jerusalem Arabs were thus kept from voting for the Knesset. For the same reason, the Israelis refused to allow the Arabs of East Jerusalem to participate in the political process in the territories, a process that the Israelis themselves had initiated. As a result, the participation of the Arabs of East Jerusalem was the major point of contention in the negotiations over elections in the territories, and over the composition of the Jordanian-Palestinian delegation to the Madrid peace talks. The Israelis granted the residents of East Jerusalem the right to vote in municipal elections, and in fact a few thousand exercised this right—but they could vote only for Jewish parties.

The Israelis needed only self-legitimation. According to them, the main thing was that they themselves believed in the legitimacy of the annexation, since all Jerusalem belonged to them by historical right. What was no less important was that the members of their community believed that their rule was just and fair. The Arab rebellion led them to feel that the regime they had imposed was "necessitated by reality," and the absence of legitimacy thus became a convenient norm. The Arabs' expressions of rebellion (and in the absence of any means of legitimate expression, every expression of nonacceptance was rebellion) were not only a burden, they were also an asset. The crisis of legitimacy and violence did not threaten the regime, but rather increased the cohesiveness of the Jewish collective and its support of the regime. The government demanded "law and order" and condemned violations, but it simultaneously benefited from the institutionalization of the crisis, which justified the use of force and of enforcement measures that did not fit the accepted criteria of a democratic state. Moreover, concern for "rule of law" replaced concern for "the legitimacy of the law." In other words, the distinction was blurred between "the rule of law" as a concept embodying universal, liberal, and democratic norms of government, and "rule through law," which is nothing but a unilateral, coercive system of enforcement.

Democratic-liberal societies are distinguished by the high correlation between political power and legitimacy. The regime depends on the identification of the majority of its subjects with its authority. The political-administrative system functions in accordance with unchallengeable principles, or at least principles the majority feels should be protected from challenge. Of course, in such societies there are sharp social conflicts and deep ideological divisions, but all these are conducted efficiently within the political system. A two-party or multiparty system allows the transfer of power from one group to another in an orderly manner, and alternating coalitions of civic groups ensure that government power never remains permanently in the hands of one group. Under such conditions, any attempt to act against the basic principles of the regime, or to topple it by force, is illegitimate. Such attempts are countered with the full force of the law, and freedoms and the rules of the democratic game may even be suspended in emergencies. Ironically, the more solid the democratic tradition, the harder it is to deal with the basic challenge that the crisis of legitimacy poses. Regimes based on coercion do not ask their subjects for legitimation and are not bothered by the contradiction between the values of democratic society and a regime imposed on a subject population.

Of course, it is possible to argue that a democratic society will never encounter a crisis of legitimacy, because it would never annex a hostile population against its will. A democratic society will not persevere in a situation of imposed rule, but will grant the subject population the right of self-determination. There are, however, situations—and the situation in Jerusalem is a clear example—in which a democratic society is motivated and acts in accordance with imperatives that it considers absolute and of greater importance than democratic-universal values. For the Israelis, Jerusalem is fundamental to their identity as a nation and country, and their control of it symbolizes their control of their own destiny and their ability to determine their future. They see these values as absolute, so any concession is perceived as a threat to their survival as a nation. The price they pay—physical insecurity and loss of life, not to mention ideological dissonance—is for them a reasonable one. Their superior rights as a collective, their unilateral approach and advancement of their own interests—and, therefore, discrimination against the dominated population—are based on a feeling that their demands regarding Jerusalem exclude all other rights, national or democratic. For this reason, the Israeli regime in Jerusalem is particular and not universal, and the subordinate position of the minority causes no ideological tension. Universal principles and the democratic system do not cross the ethnic divide. Most Israelis see their national demands as a sufficiently solid justification for basic inequality and the imposition of their rule.

Bothered by the insoluble contradiction between patriotic and democratic values, liberal Israelis sought to escape it by defining the problem in terms of civil rights, seeing the conflict as the struggle of a deprived minority ("second-class citizens") for a larger slice of the public pie. This approach could be taken so long as the Arabs were in the stage of sporadic rebellion, when many of them were indeed concerned with raising their standard of living. But the minute the Arabs' mobilization reached critical mass and the Intifada broke out, it was no longer possible to adhere to an apolitical agenda and to continue to define the problem as one of individual discrimination. Israelis gave up the attempt to create a system of relations that would moderate conflict in a noncoercive way and put their faith in the ability of the security forces to impose order.

The classic role of the government is a double one—first, to supply services and to apportion public resources; and second, to resolve or manage conflicts between citizen groups. The Israeli governmental system in Jerusalem does not apportion public resources in an equal or rational way; neither does it resolve or manage the intercommunal conflict. It is itself an inseparable part of the conflict, helping to inflame it. The regime openly discriminates against the Arab population with regard to services, allotment of resources, licensing, and environmental development. Of the huge development funds that the government ministries spend on the construction of neighborhoods and on infrastructural development, the Jewish sector gets 95 percent and the Arab sector only 5 percent.

Ironically, while Jerusalem's municipal leaders advocated coexistence, tolerance, and civil equality, the city invested a smaller portion of its development budget in the Arab sector than the central government did. In 1986, the year before the outbreak of the Intifada, the city invested only 3 percent of the total municipal development budget in East Jerusalem. This declined to 2.6 percent in 1990. In an interview that Teddy Kollek gave immediately after the Temple Mount massacre, he acknowledged the discrimination: "I've done something for Jewish Jerusalem in the past twenty-five years; for East Jerusalem? Nothing!" Moreover, land confiscation for "public purposes" in Jerusalem means taking lands from Arabs and giving it to Jews. About 40 percent of the area annexed to Israel was confiscated from its Arab owners in order to provide for the settlement of more than 180,000 Jews.

This expropriation is sometimes accomplished under the guise of "security requirements." Buildings seized for reasons of "security and public order" were handed over to groups of Jewish extremists, who turned them into bases for harassing Arabs. When the Arabs reacted, it provided an excuse for further seizures—"for security purposes." Government agencies earmarked public funds for the "Judaization" of the Muslim quarter of the Old City and the purchase of houses in Arab neighborhoods. The government was not ashamed to use the cheapest legal tricks to get possession of Arab property. Supporters of Greater Israel defined people living on the West Bank as "residents of an enemy territory" and confiscated their property in Jerusalem, which was then handed over to Jews on the grounds that the owners were "absent." An Arab resident of the Old City's Jewish Quarter who tried to repurchase the home that had been confiscated from him was turned away. A High Court of Justice ruling on his case stated: "There is no improper discrimination in the designation of these quarters [Jewish, Muslim, Christian and Armenian] for specific communities."

Yet groups of Jews who settled in the heart of Arab neighborhoods received massive government aid and police protection, since "it is inconceivable that Jews not be able to live anywhere in united Jerusalem, the heart of the [national] consensus." At the

beginning of 1992, immediately after the Madrid peace conference, and during the last months of the Likud government, there
was a concentrated effort to "Judaize" East Jerusalem. Making
use of regulations for the expedition of construction that were
enacted in order to accelerate the absorption of Russian immi-
grants, the government rushed through plans for hundreds of
dwellings in what were, in terms of planning, the most sensitive
places—in the visual basin of the Old City. With government
encouragement, groups of zealots "invaded" Arab buildings in
the city of David. Government officials forged ownership deeds,
encouraged witnesses to perjure themselves, and budgeted
unlimited funds for the "operation." The dimensions of the plunder and the injustices suffered by Arab residents were revealed
after the fall of the Likud and the establishment of a Labor government under Yitzhak Rabin. A panel of experts uncovered the
"negligence," returned some property to its owners, and canceled
outrageous plans. Still, the Jews already settled in the heart of
Arab areas remained where they were. The daily friction was not
eliminated, and this led to chronic violence.

Much thought and money have been invested in fostering
symbols and festivities whose purpose is to adorn Jewish rule in
Jerusalem with the mantle of legitimacy, the most prominent
being the Jerusalem unification celebrations every year on the
28th of the Hebrew month of Iyar (May–June), the anniversary
of the conquest of the eastern city in the 1967 Six-Day War.
Raising the legitimacy of Jewish rule to the level of ideology,
these mass celebrations combine religious and nationalist events
with entertainment programs, prayers of thanks, and memorial
ceremonies for the soldiers who fell in the war. It is an opportu-

nity to make extremist political declarations; the thousands of participants in the annual Jerusalem march affirm their "allegiance to the united city, Israel's capital, ours forever and ever."

The Jerusalem Unification Day celebrations gain momentum in direct proportion to the increasing feeling that the city is divided along an ethnic fault line. Groups and individuals who are generally afraid to visit the Old City and to pray at the Western Wall assemble there by the tens of thousands on Jerusalem Day and traverse East Jerusalem's passageways—an impassioned crowd, shouting slogans, watched over by soldiers and policemen. The authorities—especially the Ministry for Religious Affairs and nationalist-religious bodies, but the municipality as well—invest huge sums in the event.

The institutionalization of Jerusalem Day creates an interesting comparison between it and Israel's Independence Day, the 5th of Iyar (May 14). The hidden competition between the two national anniversaries goes beyond the narrow Jerusalem context, marking an ideological divide between two political cultures struggling for the soul of the Jewish Israeli collective. This is a struggle between the State of Israel—an entity that functions according to liberal Western criteria, and membership in which is determined by citizenship—and the Land of Israel—an entity in which tribal-fundamentalist values rule, and membership in which is tested by adherence to Judaism in its religious-traditional or patriotic-nationalist sense.

Not everyone is party to the promotion of Jerusalem Day. Many view it as a chauvinistic, divisive symbol, a mere reminder of Israel's illegal annexation of Arab Jerusalem. Yet in this they fall wide of historical truth. The 28th of Iyar 5727 was indeed a decisive historical event of a kind rare even in the eventful chronicle of an ancient nation such as the people of Israel. What matters is not the meaning people try to attach to it, but the fact that it opened a new era and created an irreversible historical dynamic. The physical unification of the city set powerful processes in motion, and these changed the face and character of Jerusalem beyond recognition. These processes have positive and negative effects, just like every other human action. It is impossible, however, to deny that what once was will never be again. It was largely the Jewish citizens of the city who benefited from this unification of the city, but there was also a huge improvement in Arab citizens' quality of life. This is the reason that all citizens of Jerusalem, both Jewish and Arab, support the physical unification of the city, and the debate has involved only the character of the political arrangements that will satisfy the different national affiliations.

One may, then, compare the Jewish "return" to Jerusalem to the Declaration of Independence—but there is one important difference. Independence Day, among nonreligious Jews, is perceived as the symbol of Jewish redemption; many religious circles, however, have trouble thinking of the establishment of a secular state as "the beginning of redemption" in its traditional sense. The liberation of the nation's holy places removed all doubt that the state and its army were the finger of God. In this way the unification of Jerusalem was an experience that jolted the entire Jewish nation, religious and secular alike. This common experience was what laid the foundations for "Greater Israel," and is what sustains nationalist-religious zealots in their attempt to overwhelm Jerusalem.

Among the collective for whom liberation meant subordination, however, the "return" awakened a sense of loss, whose force should not be minimized. The Intifada and the growing force of nationalist-fundamentalist emotions among the Arab population are the ultimate expressions of this "loss." Thus, on the anniversary of the unification of Jerusalem, two communities permeated with the nationalist-religious fervor unique to the human collectives that share it confront each other, and the confrontation exacerbates tribal urges, hatred, and alienation.

It was precisely the dispute over symbols and attempts to establish the legitimacy of Israeli rule that led Israelis to unite around the personality of Mayor Teddy Kollek. Like other local authorities in Israel, the Jerusalem municipality has little influence over the actions of the central government, especially in matters of supreme national importance, such as the affairs of Israel's capital. Unwilling to share any glory, government ministries have insisted on direct involvement in determining demographic, geographic, and economic realities in Jerusalem. Despite this, Israel's rule over Jerusalem was identified with Teddy Kollek for more than twenty-eight years. Kollek's charisma is the nucleus around which the ideological legitimation of Israel's rule took form and came to be accepted by the entire Jewish public.

Jerusalem has always been a battleground for seekers of absolute truth: "Sons of Light" determined to massacre the "Sons of Darkness" in the name of universal love. Likewise, this ancient, beautiful city on the border of the wilderness has always been the home of prophets of doom and seekers of justice striving to exercise their inalienable rights no matter what the cost. Teddy Kollek tried to impose on Jerusalem the harmonious, rounded worldview he brought with him from Vienna, the city of his childhood. As a boy he experienced the death throes of the ancient multinational Hapsburg empire. As a teenager he was exposed to the spectacular cultural flowering of the 1920s. As a young man, he was a firsthand witness to the bloody, catastrophic struggle between the Nazi "national myth" and the "revolutionary vision" of the socialists. Kollek believed that what had failed in central Europe, rent as it was with ancient ethnic hatreds, would succeed in Jerusalem. He believed that the power of his optimism would glue together the city's anguished residents, and that time was on his side.

Kollek is not a man of words, so he hoped to make his influence felt through his actions, to divert his citizens' minds from their daily difficulties and to persuade them that there was a good life beyond their destructive hatred. He is not a naive man—he had no illusions—but his harmonic worldview did not allow him to grasp the reality in terms of a primeval shepherds' war that in and of itself contained no solution. Abhorring insoluble enigmas, he defined things according to his ability to supply an answer. He left the question of "sovereignty" and the demands of "divine right" to the bigots and politicians. He was content to cope with the symptoms of the malaise and to try to help people live with the problem, hoping that time would eventually create a situation more susceptible to solution.

This pragmatic, optimistic approach won the hearts of all. The stern, fanatical city, saturated with tragedy, demanded a comforter, not a Jeremiah; a healer rather than a surgeon's scalpel. People wanted solace, wanted to feel that they were good, tolerant, and liberal, while pursuing their own particularist interests. Teddy Kollek gave them a cloak of respectability that hid the contradiction between their deeds and their self-image. When he was asked whether he didn't feel that he was serving as a fig leaf for the government's policy of dispossession, he answered: "Yes, I feel

that way sometimes, but what else can I do? It serves Jerusalem."
Kollek's willingness to serve Jerusalem was greatly exploited by
those who worked tirelessly to impose an Israeli version of a
united Jerusalem; the good-hearted liberals, in contrast, believed
that so long as he was mayor, not all was lost.

Jerusalem demands that its mayor take three fundamental but
contradictory approaches to his job. Firstly, he must be a zeal-
ous patriot who gives preference to the interests of his community and who pursues them resolutely; secondly, he must be a
professional go-getter who can operate an honest administration
and allocate resources in a rational way; thirdly, he must be a
compromiser and peacemaker who relaxes tensions and manages
conflicts—an impartial arbitrator. The Israeli public wished to
see Teddy Kollek as a man who was wise enough to function in
all three, contradictory roles; and, in fact, in his activity, and
especially in his words, all three approaches were expressed.

At times he made nationalist, even sharply xenophobic declarations, such as "I wouldn't want an Arab to live on my street."
Sometimes he emphasized that he acted without bias or preju-
dice, and that the city's development policy was totally egalitarian: "I received 100,000 tulip bulbs and I'm planting them
equally on the two sides of the city." Sometimes he emphasized
the need to moderate conflicts and search for consensual political
solutions: "In order to keep the peace and maintain justice in
Jerusalem, we must go beyond the cliché of sovereignty, beyond
the fears and preconceptions that drive nations to go to war, and
look for new forms of freedom and political structures."

The problem was neither contradictory approaches nor
Kollek's actions, but the erroneous impression that Teddy Kollek
headed the governmental system in Jerusalem, when, in fact, no

such unified body existed. Many government ministries function in Jerusalem, competing with and acting against one another; the municipal government is weaker than any of them. Each sees itself as advancing Israeli interests, refuses to rationalize allocations of resources and ignores the need to equalize services. For the most part, they have inflamed the Jewish-Arab conflict rather than trying to solve or even manage it.

Teddy Kollek's image as Jerusalem's leader was convenient for these ministries, since it ensured public support and world sympathy and allowed them to act in an atmosphere of optimal public relations. Accordingly, they overlooked Kollek's sharp criticism of them when they made especially extreme moves. They knew that the mayor had to believe in his own myth of coexistence and could never concede that extremism had called it into question. Kollek stood by the myth both when ministries and officials caused severe provocations and when the Palestinians defied Israeli rule. Six years after the start of the Intifada, Kollek continued to declare his faith that it was possible to find a consensual solution in the framework of the status quo of the imposed regime. He claimed that his error was only a matter of scheduling: "I thought that it [Arab acquiescence] would come more quickly. Now I think that it might take 100 years." The Jewish public continued to believe this last optimist, since without the words of comfort he voiced they would have to confront an insoluble reality. But the gap between myth and reality caused Kollek great frustration. Because of the challenge to the image of peaceful coexistence, which was entirely identified with him personally, he felt that the violence and provocations were directed specifically at him. For Kollek, the Intifada was a personal insult.

Anger at the Arabs' ingratitude, along with the burden of age, contributed to Kollek's diminished interest in the Arab population. In the elections of 1994, Kollek had to rely on Arab voters to offset the Jewish ultra-orthodox votes promised to his right-wing opponent Ehud Olmert. The Arabs, however, found no reason to participate in elections to a city government that did almost nothing for them. Only 8,000 out of 100,000 eligible Arab voters cast their votes. By their abstention Arabs indicated that they saw no difference between Kollek and his opponent: both pursued partisan Jewish policies; the former simply disguised them under a thick layer of liberal rhetoric, while the latter preferred blunt chauvinistic statements to satisfy his followers.

Kollek lost, and his demise ushered in a new era of polarization in Jerusalem that coincided and clashed with a new era of conciliation in Israeli-Palestinian relationships. The right-wing, ultra-orthodox ruling coalition in the municipal government represented two-thirds of Jerusalem's Jewish population. By its actions and statements, which included active support of Jewish intrusion into Arab neighborhoods, financial aid to zealot fringe groups, and agitation against the peace process, it involved the municipality in the ongoing political dispute and exacerbated friction with the Arab population. It represented the real attitudes of the majority of the Jewish population, hidden for so long beneath the liberal mantle of Teddy Kollek.

In a poll conducted in November 1977, Jewish respondents were asked: "What is the largest concession that you would be willing to make with regard to East Jerusalem in order to reach a peace treaty with the Arabs?" One percent of those asked were willing to return East Jerusalem to Jordan; 2 percent were willing to return it to Jordan on condition that Israelis could live in the ceded territory; 21 percent were willing to establish an Israeli-Jordanian condominium; 76 percent said that Jerusalem should remain under exclusive Israeli control, come what may. In November 1990, the proportion of those unwilling to compromise on Jerusalem under any circumstances had increased to 89 percent, while the number of those willing to consider compromise of any kind fell to 11 percent.

This trend is the reverse of that revealed in other polls on possible concessions in the occupied territories. There seems to be a greater willingness to consider territorial compromise in the West Bank. It is easy enough to explain the contradiction, however. Israelis have been accustomed to view Jerusalem as an integral part of the State of Israel. Israeli control of Jerusalem is considered legitimate, and exclusive control of it embodies Jews' aspirations to independence and control of their destiny. No one has presented Israelis with the inevitable need to choose between peace and exclusive control of Jerusalem. On the contrary, those who have dared suggest such a thing have been condemned as traitors. Israelis believe that they can achieve peace and keep Jerusalem united. "The territories," an undefined area, are ostensibly a different matter. There is some willingness to agree to territorial compromise in the West Bank, albeit undefined, inasmuch as such a position requires no immediate decision about what is to be ceded.

The escalation of tension in Jerusalem did not sharpen the need to present realistic alternatives demanding immediate political decisions to the city's Jewish and Arab citizens. But the intensification of the conflict encouraged a renewed wave of theoretical solutions, and in this Jerusalem's problem was no different from other violent conflicts.

Political enigmas excite the imaginations of people as if they were unscaled mountain peaks. As the difficulties grow, so does the desire to meet the challenge; as the object proves elusive, facing the challenge becomes a goal in and of itself, and the declaration of a willingness to confront it becomes more important than achieving the goal itself. Since 1917, when Jerusalem became a pressing international problem, no fewer than forty plans and proposals have been suggested. Despite this, the problem has not been resolved: in fact, it has become more severe. The slight chance that any mutually acceptable solution may be found, and the low probability that a compromise plan may be accepted, have only encouraged, rather than deterred, the planners.

It is truly astounding how much intellectual effort has been expended and how much goodwill has been evinced in attempts to solve the Jerusalem problem. The documents, explanatory notes, protocols, and maps fill shelves upon shelves. Among them are—to name but a few—the Sykes-Picot plan of 1916, the Arlosoroff plan of 1933, the Peel Commission plan of 1936, the Woodhead Commission plan of 1938, the Fitzgerald plan of 1945, the UN Commission plan (majority and minority) of 1947, the UN General Assembly resolution on 1947, the Count Bernadotte proposals of 1948, the Trusteeship Commission plan of 1950, the Vatican Proposals of 1948–80, the Conciliation Commission of the UN, the Rogers plan, King Hussein's federation plan of 1972, the various Israeli proposals dating from 1967 (including this author's Borough Plan), the Sadat proposal of 1978, and Quaker, Swedish, Dutch, and Palestinian proposals.

Despite differences in the level of sophistication and detail of the various plans, there is a great deal of similarity in the solutions they propose. When the proposals are placed side by side, strange congruities are revealed, of which the authors were generally unaware. The similarities are not coincidental. The planners understood the complexity of the Jerusalem problem and endeavored, each in their own ways, to address the three components of the problem: sovereignty, the holy sites, and municipal government.

The conflict over Jerusalem is generally perceived in its political-international context. It is defined as a struggle for sovereignty that will be resolved when a mutually acceptable arrangement is made with regard to who is sovereign in the Holy City, or how sovereignty is to be divided between the two national communities to which Jerusalem is home. Since the problem of Jerusalem is the focal point of the struggle over the land between the Jordan and the Mediterranean, a solution for Jerusalem depends, however, on a solution for the land as a whole.

The centrality of the sovereignty problem and the emotional baggage accompanying it overshadow two other complex problems—on the one hand, the question of the holy sites and interreligious conflict, and on the other, the question of municipal government and local ethnic competition. These questions are intertwined with the sovereignty question, but are not identical to it. Even after a sovereignty arrangement is found, the conflicts between Jews, Muslims, and the Christian communities will not disappear, and neither will the dissension between Jews and Arabs over positions in the municipal administration and over the allocation of resources cease. Israelis who adhere to their desired solution—absolute and indivisible Israeli sovereignty—prefer to emphasize the secondary problems and obscure the sovereignty problem. Accordingly, they propose plans meant to ensure self-administration of the holy places and freedom for all religions. They also suggest decentralization of municipal government, granting municipal autonomy to minorities.

These proposals contain nothing new. The principle of non-interference in the holy places was established as early as the League of Nations Mandate for Palestine, and the division of the city into ethnic-based submunicipalities was proposed in 1933 by Chaim Arlosoroff. These proposals are made, of course, because they are consistent with the principle of absolute Israeli sovereignty. Unfortunately, in holding to this principle, the Israelis are trying to avoid the kernel of the problem, the question of sovereignty. As a result, these proposals cannot end the conflict, because it is not religious and local, but national and general.

Non-Israeli forces—Arabs and others—wish to solve the sovereignty problem via political partition, the classic solution of international conflicts, moving the boundary lines that absolutely define the limits of each side's sovereignty, while nonetheless preserving the physical unity of Jerusalem. Knowing that this solution cannot be applied to the Old City, they propose removing it from the bounds of the national conflict, making it a universal Holy City. They emphasize that the Old City amounts to only 1 percent of the entire municipal territory called Jerusalem. These approaches are not new either. Satisfying the national aspirations of Jews and Arabs through the internationalization of Jerusalem's symbolic sites was the basis of the Peel Commission plan of 1936, the Jerusalem internationalization plan of 1947, the Conciliation Commission plan of 1949, and other proposals.

It is difficult, if not impossible, however, to carry out a political partition while preserving Jerusalem's physical unity. Furthermore, the attempt to apply the principle of universality to the Old City has been rejected by both sides. The attempt to isolate the religious component is realistic, perhaps, with regard to the Church of the Holy Sepulchre, but it cannot be applied to the Western Wall and the mosques on the Temple Mount, which are no less national symbols than religious ones.

These well-meaning, disinterested intellectual efforts have not done much more than rehash old ideas in more sophisticated form. The problem is not a need for theoretical solutions but the willingness of the two sides to use the available plans as tools for resolving the conflict. The conventional wisdom accepted by all sides is that there is no solution to the sovereignty question at present; there seems to be no way to bridge the gulf between the Israeli and Palestinian positions, and this being the case, it seems better to postpone tackling the stumbling block of Jerusalem until a later stage of the negotiations.

Isolating the problem of Jerusalem fails, however, because a serious dialogue inevitably involves issues that have implications for the city. Moreover, an attempt to isolate Jerusalem may be construed as supporting the Israeli position that it is an integral part of Israel, not occupied territory. While it is accepted that problems specific to Jerusalem should be treated only in the last phase of the negotiations, on the final disposition of the territories, there is no agreement on one crucial matter: what is Jerusalem? In other words, to what geographical areas would the special status apply?

According to the Israelis, the area of Jerusalem is delimited by the municipal boundary established in 1967 (see Map 1). This encompasses almost 20,000 acres, on which giant Jewish neighborhoods have been built, housing more than 180,000 residents, as well as the homes of more than 160,000 Palestinians. The

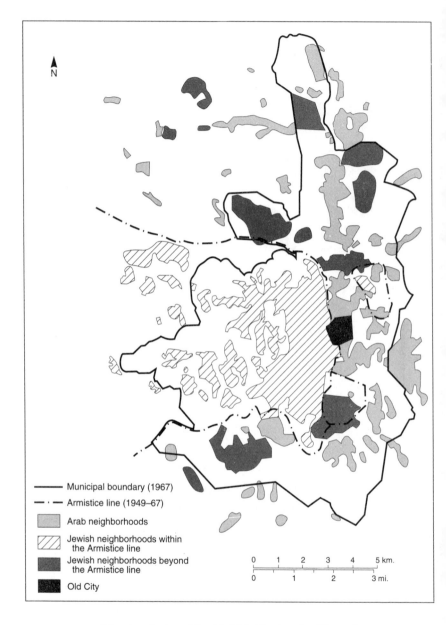

N

Municipal boundary (1967)
Armistice line (1949–67)
Arab neighborhoods
Jewish neighborhoods within
the Armistice line
Jewish neighborhoods beyond
the Armistice line
Old City

0   1   2   3   4   5 km.
0   1   2   3 mi.

Map 1.   Arab and Jewish Neighborhoods of Jerusalem

Palestinians, however, who do not recognize the 1967 annexation, define Jerusalem as the area under the jurisdiction of the last Jordanian municipality—the Old City and the adjacent areas—less than 10 percent of the area claimed by Israel. The rest, including Mount of Olives, Beit Hanina, most Palestinian neighborhoods, and especially the new Jewish neighborhoods, are considered part of the West Bank. According to the Palestinians, the Jewish residents are "settlers," and the Palestinian residents form an integral part of the population of the West Bank. The Palestinians maintain that all arrangements applied to the West Bank automatically apply to the area outside the Old City and its immediate environs.

Not satisfied with the existing municipal boundaries, the Israelis wish to expand "Greater Jerusalem" in ever-widening circles. National consensus legitimizes concerted efforts to build houses and pave highways outside the municipal boundaries. The effort to integrate the hinterland and create one continuous Jewish presence coincides with an attempt to cut off Arab residents of Jerusalem from Arabs living on the West Bank. This policy of integration, as far as the Israelis are concerned, and separation, as far as the Palestinians are concerned, characterizes the prevailing conditions in and around Jerusalem—a sure recipe for friction and animosity.

CHAPTER TWO

BORDER OR FRONTIER?

There is something pathetic about Israel's attempt to divorce Jerusalem's reality from its immediate geographic, social, and political context. Everything points to the explicit, inseparable link between life in the city and in its hinterland. It is the big city at the center of the West Bank's economic, political, and social life. It is impossible to pass through the West Bank without crossing Jerusalem. The area's transportation systems and infrastructure are all concentrated in Jerusalem or pass through it. With an area of some 200 square miles, four times that of Jerusalem itself, the metropolitan region outside the municipal border is home to 180,000 Palestinians and 50,000 Jews, and almost all of these find themselves in the city each day, at work or for other daily needs. Those who come to the city and are not aware of the Israeli frame of mind would never imagine that the united city, in its official borders, belongs to "another country," not to the area surrounding it, and that its relations with its immediate periphery are "extrinsic."

The Israelis, however, take this artificial separation seriously. Since Jerusalem is an inseparable part of Israel's sovereign territory, it is not under military rule. This means that the police force, rather than the army, is responsible for the city's security; only men in police uniform are responsible for law and order there. When a closure is imposed on the territories—in other words, when Arab inhabitants of the territories are forbidden to enter Israel—the main roads leading to Jerusalem are blocked and Palestinians are not allowed to traverse them, even on their way from the northern to the southern West Bank. They cannot open their businesses in the city, reach the hospitals within its limits, or pray in the mosques on the Temple Mount. Entry into Israel by residents of the territories is considered a security risk, yet the Palestinians of East Jerusalem can move freely throughout the city and the country in their cars.

Israel's attempt to pry Jerusalem away from the territories has a macabre tinge to it because of the absurd borders created in 1967. The considerations used in determining the area to be annexed derived from the aspiration to include "a maximum of land with a minimum of Arabs." The city limit itself was determined by military-tactical considerations, since the sense at the time was that sooner or later, the rest of the West Bank would end up under the rule of another country. Army officers demarcated the border so that it would "remove the city from the danger of artillery shelling." The northernmost point of the border was set just south of a distillery for the manufacture of arak, an anise-flavored liquor popular throughout the Levant. The reasoning was that "its products should be marketed in the West Bank and not in Israel." For the same reason, the eastern border was drawn to keep out a cigarette factory. Mayor Teddy Kollek wanted a municipal airport, so the new borders included the small airport at Atarot and the road leading to it.

The densely populated Arab suburbs to the east of the road were, however, left outside the border. The border became absurd when densely populated neighborhoods sprang up around the city and nearby Arab towns and villages grew until they became contiguous with neighborhoods in the city. Between the years 1967 and 1987, the Palestinian population of the area around the annexed land doubled, the same rate of growth enjoyed by the Arab population within the municipal border. Many of the city's Palestinian residents, carrying Israeli identity cards, could not find space to build homes within the city, partly because Israel expropriated 40 percent of the entire annexed area. They left the city for the periphery, where they built some twenty thousand homes. For twenty-two years they were not bothered by their "displacement" to the West Bank, and no one made its implications clear to them. The rights granted them as residents of the State of Israel, specifically social security allowances, were not withdrawn, and neither were their freedom of movement and their freedom to cross into Jerusalem impeded.

It was only during the twenty-third year of the occupation that they realized what a mistake they had made. A police force arrived at the junction that led out of "Israeli territory" and put up earthworks that blocked these people's way into town. They were forced to take a long detour via the roadblocks; there they were checked just like all other West Bankers who wished to enter Israel. There were thousands of people whose official residence, according to population records, was in the West Bank, but who resided with their families in Jerusalem. These were required to "go home"; when they were caught they were sent to the towns where they were registered and forbidden to live with their spouses and children. When army personnel were asked why they were making the daily lives of these Palestinians so difficult, the answer was: "It is inconceivable that in Jerusalem, of all places, there be a security risk because no one controls the entry of West Bank residents." Yet no one dared to set up roadblocks within the city, between the Arab and Jewish neighborhoods, to make it hard for Jerusalem Arabs planning to attack Jews. "Such a step would mean the division of the city," they said.

The separation of Jerusalem from the territories raised political and ideological problems as well. The advocates of Greater Israel ridiculed the absurd borders established by the Labor party government in 1967; in 1990, Benyamin Begin, a member of the Knesset, called them "the arak and cigarette borders." For them, there is no difference between the territory annexed to Israel and the rest of Judea and Samaria; both are the land of the Jewish forefathers.

Paradoxically, it was the devotees of territorial compromise who sanctified the annexation lines, giving ex post facto sanction to the restrictions on the movement of Arabs and other aspects of the imposed separation. They saw the police roadblocks and the system of entry permits as a "resuscitation" of the Green Line—and, as such, as the first step toward "a territorial compromise." "The entry permits are like visas required at every border," one of them said.

The Greater Israel enthusiasts did not, of course, protest the separation and heavy-handed treatment of the Arabs. On the contrary, they wanted all the draconian measures used on the West Bank to be applied in Jerusalem as well. It infuriated them that Israeli law, in force in Jerusalem, does not allow for the deportation of Palestinians and administrative detention without judicial review, as in the territories. Of course, the champions of Greater Israel were also the first to denounce any attempt to infringe on any of these same laws when the targets were Jews. Their scorn for the 1967 annexation borders coexisted with holy reverence for the term "Greater Jerusalem." Anyone who dared speculate about the possibility of contracting the borders was denounced as a traitor.

The advocates of territorial compromise were upset, needless to say, by the severe measures imposed by the Israeli government and considered them to be violations of civil rights, but they could not come up with any alternative. Most of them supported Israeli rule over a united Jerusalem and wanted to let their patriotic feelings for their capital city run free. Yet they also wanted the status of the rest of the territories to be open to negotiation. The geographic and legal distinction between the territories under military rule and Jerusalem was crucial to their worldview, and they could not but view the measures used to enforce the separation through their particular ideological prism.

Of course, the attempts to evade reality have not been successful. Those who wished to put a positive gloss on the steps enforcing the separation ran up against an unresolvable contradiction between the reality they would like to see and the reality they were confronted with. The Arabs were the first to testify to the absurdity of the Israeli viewpoint. As far as they were concerned, there was no difference between an Israeli in a blue policeman's uniform and a soldier in a green army uniform. At the beginning of the Intifada, it looked as if the police force were operating under less severe rules than the army was, but the gap was closed when Border Guard forces were deployed under police command in Jerusalem, using the same infamous methods they used in the West Bank. The Palestinians in Jerusalem engaged in the same acts of rebellion and protest that were seen in the territories, and violent incidents were no less frequent in the city than in the territories. It would seem that just as the Israelis wished to emphasize that Jerusalem had been detached from the territories, the Palestinians wished to prove that the city was an inseparable part of occupied Palestine.

In 1984, some 21,000 Jews resided within Jerusalem's commuting area outside the municipal borders, within a radius of thirty minutes' travel from the city. About half of them lived in Ma'aleh Adumim, a suburb along the road to Jericho, and the rest in the area stretching from Beit El to the north to Gush Etzion in the south. By 1987, their number had grown to 30,000. When the Intifada began, and stones and Molotov cocktails were frequently thrown at Jewish vehicles, many saw this as the end of the settlements. Who would dare endanger his family and settle in such risky places?

The growth of the Jewish population on Jerusalem's periphery did in fact slow down, but by 1989, the Intifada had become a way of life, and its dangers did not outweigh the advantages of moving out to the suburbs. Occasional acts of violence could not offset the financial incentives showered on the inhabitants of these areas and the prospect of an affordable dream house with lawn. Market forces pushed young couples out of the crowded city center into suburbs with a high standard of living and good public services that were not too far from employment and entertainment.

According to surveys, about a third of the Jews who left Jerusalem during the 1980s moved into the metropolitan area to the west and east. This relocation was only residential; the great majority continued to work in the city. A network of bypass roads shortened travel time into the city center and minimized the danger of attacks on Jewish vehicles. At the end of 1994, about 12,500 Jewish families, some 55,000 people, were living in the metropolitan area outside the municipal borders.

In 1991, toward the end of the Likud administration, an ambitious zoning plan was prepared, setting aside lands in the "territories" beyond Jerusalem's city limits for the creation of some 60,000 residential units—enough to house 300,000 Jews. It embodied an element of fantasy, since the average annual population growth rate in the 1980s fluctuated at around 8–12 percent. But the political significance of the plan lay not in the number of housing units planned but in the amount of land reserved by a statutory zoning plan as "land for the expansion of settlements."

These large parcels of land have become a major point of dispute in the negotiations for Palestinian self-government; in fact, they may prove to be an obstacle impossible to overcome. The building starts launched by the Likud government in the territories were frozen or drastically curtailed by the Labor government under Yitzhak Rabin. But this did not affect the Jerusalem metropolitan area, because all the suburbs in that area are defined by Labor's platform as "security settlements." The ideology of Greater Israel was exchanged for security considerations. The new administration considered the Jewish settlements around the city to be Greater Jerusalem's defense line. The aura of legitimacy supplied by Jerusalem was thus expanded to include the huge 200-square-mile hinterland, some four times the municipal territory of united Jerusalem.

The Jewish settlers in the metropolitan area at the end of 1993 were some 20 percent of the total population there. Adding the Jewish and Arab population of this area to the Jewish and Arab population of the city itself shows near demographic parity between the two groups. These demographic data cast doubt on the political value of Jewish settlements on Jerusalem's periphery. What is the point of expanding the Jewish area of settlement if in doing so one must add four Arabs for every additional Jew? After all, the borders of Jerusalem were fixed in 1967 so as to ensure a Jewish majority of at least 70 percent in the city. Enlarging the area means that Jews will not have that kind of majority, and that would seem to have far-reaching political consequences.

The danger clearly presented by this demographic realignment did not, however, cause the supporters of settlement in the metropolitan area to lose any sleep. Unlike those with liberal-democratic principles, they did not see any direct, necessary connection between demography and democracy. In their view, there was nothing wrong with a permanent system of governance that gives one group full democratic rights while withholding them from another.

This dual system, which grants full political rights to Jewish settlers and local "self-rule" to the Arabs, originated in 1979. Military orders and amendments concerning Jewish local and regional councils, promulgated by the military government as "the source of authority" in the territories (in accordance with international law), made the Jewish settlements into regions in which Israeli law, justice, and administration apply without any formal annexation. The Jewish settlers moved into the occupied territories taking with them all the rights and, at least in theory, all the obligations of citizens of the State of Israel. More precisely, when they moved to the territories, they continued to enjoy all the rights, but they were not subject to all the obligations. In moving (so they were told) they fulfilled a national duty, and this made them deserving of special treatment.

At first, the size of each of these enclaves of Israeli sovereignty in the occupied territories was small, but as the settlements grew and merged into one another, these islands became blotches that spread until they grazed up against Palestinian settlements. The nature of the system was starkly transparent. The domain of free people, members of communities with self-government and well-developed public services, bordered on the realm of a subjugated people, deprived of civil rights, who lived in underdeveloped villages subject to the arbitrary whims of a hostile military regime.

Legitimization of the settlements in the occupied territories does not necessarily have its source in the ideology of Greater Israel. In the period that preceded the fall of the Likud government in 1992, there was a significant decline in the status of the settlers; fewer and fewer Israelis saw the settler movements as an expression of the realization of the Zionist dream. Many people became fed up with the fiery rhetoric of Gush Emunim, the militant religious settler movement, with the provocations committed in order to exacerbate the conflict with the Palestinians, and with the profligate waste of money on the construction of settlements, which pointedly reached fantastic proportions just after the peace conference in Madrid. The Labor party had a ready audience when it declared that it would "change priorities," in particular by freezing construction in the settlements.

With the Rabin government's assumption of power, however, it became clear that most of those who opposed the settlements and advocated territorial compromise did not, in fact, oppose all settlements. They opposed the establishment of settlements in certain areas, but they supported settlements in other regions. This distinction between areas in which settlement activity would be halted and those in which it would continue was formulated by Yitzhak Rabin, who announced that he was against "political settlements" but supported "security settlements." This is in line with his geopolitical conceptualization of the areas he wants to annex to Israel (and where, therefore, he wishes to continue Jewish settlement activity), in contrast with "densely populated Arab areas," which he wishes to turn over to Palestinian rule (and where settlement activity will be frozen). The geographic boundaries on Rabin's map leave Israel in control of the Jordan Valley and the slopes of the mountains to its west, of Gush Etzion, and of a large area around Jerusalem—the same areas included in the famous "Allon Plan" of 1968–70, except that Rabin has added large areas in western Samaria.

Labor governments had established 34 settlements in the territories. The Likud governments that followed Labor in 1977 established 85 settlements, and the "National Unity" governments in which Labor and the Likud were partners established 32 settlements. (See Map 2.) More than half the number of Jewish settlers in the occupied territories settled there during the term of the "National Unity" government. The combined effects of the pioneering ethos and the Greater Israel ideology presented the 1992 Rabin government with a settlement enterprise encompassing 137 settlements (not including military outposts), which was home to some 110,000 people.

Keeping its campaign promises, the Rabin government made a series of decisions that canceled the construction of tens of thousands of housing units mandated by the Likud government

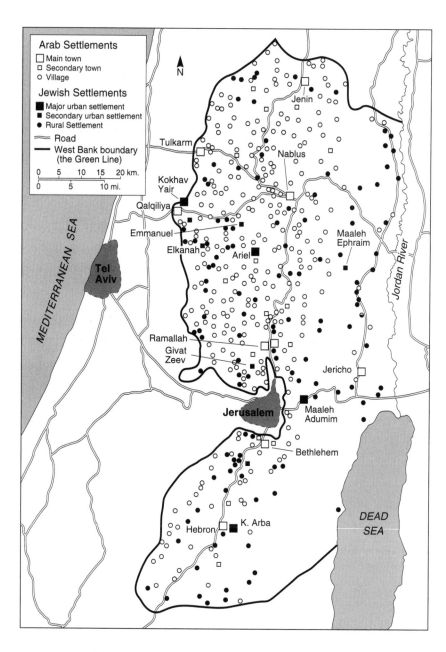

Map 2. Arab and Jewish Settlements in the West Bank

at the end of its term and froze thousands of units already under construction. It also revoked all the special tax incentives and direct subsidies to most of the West Bank settlements. The government committed itself, however, to preserving the existing settlements, specifically to continuing to provide for the settlers' security, to continuing funding of Jewish local councils, and to continuing to assume other government costs deriving from the geographical dispersion of the settlements (such as transportation for schoolchildren). Some 10,000 housing units that were in advanced stages of construction were allowed to be completed. As a result of these measures, there was a change in public attitudes, and the settlement population's annual rate of growth fell considerably, although it did not stop expanding completely.

Within Rabin's "security area," settlement activity continued. In the Jerusalem region, western Samaria, and the Jordan Valley, about 7,000 housing units were constructed with full government funding. According to the prime minister's classification, at the beginning of 1993 there were 75 Jewish "security" settlements, in which some 75,000 people lived. In contrast, there were 50 settlements containing 25,000 people defined as "political" (not including the Gaza Strip). These "security" settlements included eight of the eleven large urban centers with populations of more than 1,000. Seventy percent of the residents of the "security areas" earned their living in the large cities within Israel.

The areas reserved for the sole use of Jewish settlers are a patchwork of gray spots spread over the entire West Bank, surrounding and separating the areas of Palestinian habitation. The elimination of the continuous geopolitical line led to the drawing of another dividing line—this one human, communal, and ethnic—and each settlement has become a circle of tribal confrontation and friction. The mad boundaries drawn on the map of the West Bank anthropomorphized inanimate objects—land, trees, houses, wells—turning them into appendages of those who use them, into mute soldiers in a violent intercommunal struggle. It is as if, instead of three spatial dimensions, there were now six, with sparks flying from the points of contact between the Jewish and Arab spaces.

This ethnic division is not symmetrical, of course. The line dividing the communities is not vertical, dividing two groups of equal status, but horizontal, dividing superior and inferior groups. The Jewish settlers see themselves as the only legitimate collective in the land west of the Jordan.

Between 1949 and 1967, the geographical borders of the Jewish collective were the armistice lines established after the 1948 war. It was in this part of Palestine that the Jews established their sovereign state, and in their Declaration of Independence they defined it as "*a* Jewish State *in* the Land of Israel." With this definition they certainly emphasized the ethnic Jewish aspect of the state, and subsequent legislation confirmed the irrevocable link between the Jewish state and the Jewish people in the Diaspora. Yet this Jewish nation-state was founded on the principle of territorial sovereignty and on the formal equality of all its citizens, regardless of their ethnicity or religion.

Tension between the principle of civic equality before the law and ethnic inequality has existed in Israel since its inception. In 1967, however, when the conquest of all of Mandatory Palestine was completed, the ethnic component in Israeli political culture grew stronger, and it became clear how fragile and weak adherence to the principle of territorial sovereignty was as a governing norm in the Jewish state. When Israeli forces occupied the West Bank and Gaza, making the area under Israel's physical control greater than its sovereign territory, it became clear that the physical border of the Jewish collective was not perceived as being identical with the 1949 armistice lines. People wanted it to encompass land that had not been part of the state's sovereignty, land that stretched at least to the border of Mandatory Palestine.

It was in this context that the concept of the Jewish collective as the only legitimate community in Greater Israel was expressed. This aspiration to include the area of the former Mandatory Palestine within the borders of the Jewish collective did not arise because Jews lived in the occupied areas and wanted to merge with the Jewish sovereign state. It arose from Jews' spiritual link to their ancient homeland, despite the fact that it was now inhabited by another community, which could not and would not be able to be a legitimate part of the state of Israel. The Israelis' approach to the territory now occupied by their army was similar to the concept of the "frontier" in classic American culture: a border region beyond civilization, empty prairies inhabited by natives incapable of feeling spiritual attachment to the land and who do not constitute a legitimate collective. This idea contradicts the concept of "border" in its European sense of a boundary line separating two distinct communities, or two diverse types of human collective. The perception of Jewish ethnic attachment to the "frontier" region conquered in 1967 was immediate, and it was endorsed by all elements of the Israeli-Jewish political culture.

The annexation of Jerusalem and the settlement of the Jordan Valley in accordance with the Allon Plan were evidence of classic Zionist doctrine being applied to the occupied areas. During the first decade of Israeli occupation, the political culture of the Labor movement was in the ascendant, and its leaders remained loyal to the ideology of the founding fathers, who had tried to preserve a balance between universal-civic and particularist-ethnic values. Accordingly, they elected to restrict "the Zionist endeavor" to areas that were not actually populated by Arabs. They were prepared to reach a territorial compromise. Likewise, they saw the military administration as a temporary state of affairs, which would be terminated when a peace treaty was signed, as mandated by international law. Yet their actions and ideological rationalizations gave legitimacy to the ethnocentric approach of the Likud and of the nationalist religious parties. When Jerusalem was annexed, the minister of justice at the time, a member of the Labor party, said: "The State of Israel's judicial philosophy was always an organic perception matching the actual political facts. . . . In addition to the IDF's control, there must be a manifest sovereign act by the state. . . . The government will be authorized to determine, by order, from time to time, in what areas the state's law, justice, and administration will apply."

If the unilateral annexation of territories within the Land of Israel was a sovereign act by the government of Israel, however, why should such annexation not encompass all of Mandatory Palestine, and even territories beyond it if they fall under IDF control? If the establishment of settlements in the Jordan Valley was a Zionist endeavor, then the establishment of settlements in the "cradle of the nation"—Beit El, Hebron, and Shiloh—must be too; if acts of sovereignty are the monopoly of the Jewish collective, why shouldn't the Palestinians assume the role of "sojourners," the non-Jewish resident aliens of biblical times?

The transition from "a Jewish state in the Land of Israel"—a state with defined sovereign borders whose inhabitants enjoyed basic civic equality without ethnic classification—to "the State of Israel as the State of the Jewish People" (as it is termed by a Basic Law of 1985), in which the Jewish collective in its broadest definition has the right to establish its rule over the entire land and all its inhabitants, was slow and cumulative. As noted, all the places settled by Jewish citizens have for practical purposes been annexed to Israel by means of an elaborate web of military orders and civil legislation. Even the regime imposed on the Palestinian community on the West Bank has been radically revised by laws and procedures that the Jewish collective has an interest in implementing. Laws concerning economics, land tenure, water, legal matters, infrastructure, planning, and employment have been changed to serve Israeli interests.

Ironically, the international community viewed Israel's military rule in a positive light. Foreigners preferred to persuade themselves that this was the military administration required by international conventions governing "belligerent occupation" (the Hague Protocol and the Fourth Geneva Convention). They considered the military regime a temporary arrangement, and the alternative—Israeli annexation—a much worse option. Thus, a regime that suspended communal and political rights and violated human rights benefited from international legitimacy.

Israeli control over the Palestinians fostered the economic interests of the Jewish collective and discriminated on an ethnic basis against the subjugated population in all spheres: employment, commerce, construction, budgets, development. But the institutionalized dualism of the Israeli regime found its most pronounced expression in the monopoly the Jewish collective assumed (in accordance with orders promulgated by the military government) over the public domain, urban expansion, and symbolic assets. Civilian activity in the territories did not impose a financial burden on Israeli taxpayers; on the contrary, the taxes and levies imposed on Palestinian inhabitants of the territories were transferred for the use of the Israeli public. Lands not privately used by Palestinians and not registered in their names were declared "state lands," and as such they were given over to the exclusive use of Jewish settlers, as if the "state" in the territories were a Jewish state. When the Nablus municipality asked to enlarge its borders to relieve crowded conditions in the city (population 100,000), the administration refused under pressure from the chairman of the neighboring Jewish regional council (population 10,000). "This is state land," the council chairman argued—meaning that it had been "redeemed" for the Jewish people. Large areas under Palestinian ownership were expropriated for "public purposes" in order to pave access roads and build reservoirs and water lines for the use of the Jewish settlements. Israelis on either side of the Green Line consumed more than three-quarters of the West Bank's water potential.

The national symbols of the Palestinian collective were legally declared "inflammatory material"; the PLO was declared a "terrorist organization." Hundreds of books were on the censor's list, their very possession a crime. The universities in the territories were shut down periodically (when the Intifada broke out, they had been closed for more than four years). The line dividing the occupation army from an armed militia was always fuzzy, because the IDF, with its reserve forces, resembles a militia in many ways. Calling up settlers for police and enforcement duties in the neighboring Palestinian villages, in the framework of regular army units, did away even with appearances. To complete the picture of tribal strife, the authorities allowed Jewish settlers great latitude, including use of IDF-owned weapons and equipment. The fact that one community can appropriate to itself the regime's legitimacy, wearing its uniform and participating actively in its law-enforcement system, while the other community is defenseless and is not even recognized as a legitimate entity could not obscure the intercommunal nature of the conflict.

The intercommunal conflict that had characterized Mandatory Palestine turned into an international conflict in 1949; in 1967, however, it reverted to its original form. Under British rule, there had been two communities of equal status, each lacking access to the regime's law-enforcement system. Now there was a hierarchical society made up of a ruling collective and a subjugated one. These collectives, which had been separated by an armistice line for twenty years, had both formed their ethnic-national identities and established their physical and social borders under the British Mandate, and in 1967 the perceptions and images of the Mandate again prevailed over them. The old arguments, the fiery rhetoric, and the memory of scores of years of bloody fighting returned.

Only the lexicon of concepts adjusted itself to the new reality. The Palestinians demanded "an end to the occupation," national self-determination, and the "establishment of a national entity in any area of Palestine to be liberated," or a state within the partition borders of 1947. Despite this new phraseology, however, they continued to see the Jewish collective as an illegitimate intruder into their territory. Some of them were willing to recognize the irrefutable fact that the Jewish collective had established a power base that they could not eliminate, and that it was therefore necessary to compromise. But they did not change their position on the legitimacy of the national liberation movement of the Jewish people.

The Israelis were divided between the advocates of Greater Israel and the advocates of territorial compromise, but in fact simply renewed an old, pre-state debate about the goals of Zionism, the character of the Jewish state, and its ideological basis. The difference was, of course, that in pre-state days, the political debate had been theoretical and rhetorical, and everyone knew that it would be settled by force. Now the concepts of "partition," "binational state," "historical right," "peace," "compromise," "self-determination," and "civic equality" had immediate political significance. Now the Jewish collective could itself decide these fundamental questions and implement its decisions.

Historically, the inability of the Jewish collective to decide had been a kind of decision—the continuation of the political status quo, and with it the continuation of the exclusive rule of the Jews in a quasi-binational state. More than the status quo being a choice anchored in the ideology of Labor or the Likud, it was a decision by default. The perception that it was temporary perpetuated the political debate. Undoubtedly, were it up to the Jewish collective, the status quo would continue forever. The Israeli public has for years been in a postideological era. The ideological garb in which leaders seek to dress their conflicting political positions is no more than a means of enlisting supporters who still need ideological justifications for political mobilization. Most of the Israeli voting public is no different from the voting public in any other Western country—relatively satiated, and looking to satisfy its daily needs. Party leaders are themselves part of this public. After all, all of them reached their leadership positions from within the oligarchic, postideological bureaucracy.

The waning of the pioneer ethos, along with the opposing ethos of Greater Israel, left pure utilitarianism in its wake, a philosophy that weighs every political alternative in terms of expediency, that avoids conflicts and represses problems. Most observers agreed that a real change could be generated only by forces outside the Jewish collective, because the internal forces seeking to preserve the status quo were stronger than those seeking to change it. This was the position when, twenty years after the formation of a de facto binational state in Israel/Palestine, it was confronted with a severe challenge. The Palestinian community rose up to shake off the bonds of the Jewish ethnic regime.

CHAPTER THREE

THE UPRISING

It is conventional wisdom that the Intifada unmade the status quo of two decades of Israeli rule over the territories. "The Intifada put an end to a bad, difficult, and costly occupation," said one observer. Others asserted: "With the uprising, the Palestinians irrevocably abolished the status quo." "The Green Line was reinstated by the pitching of a stone from the hand of a Palestinian youth," declared another. Almost every analysis has defined the uprising, which began on December 9, 1987, as an anticolonial national liberation struggle. Examples: "It was an ignominious evacuation [as in the case of] powers like France from Algeria, the United States from Vietnam, and the Soviet Union from Afghanistan, after years of bloody wars of conquest." "A de-colonializing crisis." "The Israeli occupation is blindly repeating the mistakes the French made in Algeria and Indochina, the British in their colonies, and the Americans in Vietnam."

In fact, the Palestinian uprising did include all the characteristics of an anticolonial war of liberation, just as Israel's reaction evinced all the attributes of colonial repression. The violence did indeed resuscitate the Green Line—it induced the majority of Israelis to keep their distance from the West Bank and Gaza Strip. The status quo of Israeli rule characterized by minimal use of coercive force and the relative acquiescence of the subject population was over for good. Yet probing deeper results in a much more complex picture, which will be presented in two parts, the first covering the period from December 1987 until the Madrid conference in October 1991, and the second the period thereafter (Chapter 5). A survey of the causes of the uprising, its dynamics, and its place in the history of the Israeli-Palestinian conflict calls the conventional wisdom into doubt. The first concept worth examining in this context is the "status quo." What was the previous state of affairs that the Intifada changed so "irrevocably"?

It was strife, a perpetual conflict, between the Jewish Israeli and the Palestinian Arab communities. The relationship between the communities was conducted on parallel tracks of cultural and geographic segregation, of limited economic cooperation, and of physical and political confrontation. The dominant Jewish group, determined to maintain its preeminence, and the dominated Arab group, which sought to liberate itself, were locked in intercommunal strife similar to other ethnic conflicts—an endless cycle of violence, enforcement, domination, and containment. The Palestinian population of the occupied territories, rejected the legitimacy of Israeli rule and was not prepared to accept the continuation of the status quo. Twenty years of Israeli rule there had seen a notable rise in the standard of living for the Palestinians in the territories, and this had sharpened their sense of frustration and refined the expression of their protest.

Paradoxically, the Israeli occupation hastened the consolidation of the Palestinian community by presenting Palestinian society and Palestinian national identity with an acute challenge and a very serious threat. The response to this sharp challenge was equally sharp. The occupation gave birth to what seems on the face of it to be a strange situation—a community that is helpless, yet enjoys great vitality, expressed in all areas of life. This status quo was not static. The conflict erupted and subsided periodically, bounded by its internal Israeli-Palestinian framework, the geopolitical framework created in 1967, after the Israeli occupation, and encompassing the entire area of Mandatory Palestine.

The Israeli government, and especially those responsible for the military government in the territories, sought to paint a different picture of pre-Intifada conditions. They vehemently rejected the doomsday prophecies that extremism was growing and even turned a blind eye to clear indications that spontaneous violence was increasing. Some two months before the Intifada broke out, General Amram Mitzna said that fewer than one in a thousand Palestinians were involved in hostile activity, and that there were no obvious signs that spontaneous civil resistance was becoming a trend.

This view of the "static status quo" is understandable when expressed by officers who are supposed to prepare for conventional wars and who have little expertise in managing internal economic, social, and political processes. That the status quo may be regarded as stable if the conflict does not make newspaper headlines and does not touch on daily life is also comprehensible. It is not surprising that as long as it did not claim Jewish casualties, the unsolvable Palestinian problem got shunted off the public and political agenda of the Jewish population.

No wonder, then, that the status quo of two decades seemed static and stable before the Intifada. As long as Israel could hold onto the territories with limited military force and rule over two million human beings by judiciously meting out deterrents, punishment, and rewards for "positive elements," there was no reason to delve deeper into the swift, stormy processes taking place in the territories. The status quo could therefore be depicted as static, and the Intifada consequently came as a surprise, like a sudden attack. The perceived discontinuity between the old status quo and the "sudden event" of the Intifada displays a basic misunderstanding of the essence of the status quo. The use of the colonial model to explain the situation prior to the Intifada and the description of the latter as a "new type of war" are equally problematic.

The question of whether the Intifada amounts to an anticolonial national liberation struggle seems rhetorical: what could be more colonial than the occupation of the West Bank and Gaza Strip? A country occupies a territory that is not its own, settles its citizens there, monopolizes its natural resources, and creates economic dependency based on the exploitation of the natives' cheap labor and on a market that protects the industrial output of the mother country. This colonialism is enforced by an army of occupation from the mother country, and it persists so long as the mother country can impose its rule. An anticolonial war of liberation, the Intifada, leads to inability to control the territory. As a result, the colonial power dismantles its governing apparatus and evacuates its army and settlers back to the mother country.

Upon careful examination, however, this model is problematic. For example, a colonial model presumes that the borders of the mother country are defined: how, then, can one understand a situation in which half the mother country's capital is in the mother country and half is a colony? Not every case in which one nation rules another is colonial. The occupation of Afghanistan by the Soviet Union and American involvement in Vietnam, as well as the suppression of the freedom movements in Hungary and Czechoslovakia by the Soviet Union, were not colonial. White minority rule in South Africa and the presence of British military forces in Northern Ireland cannot simplistically be defined as colonial situations either. Other models of domination may be more appropriate to define Israel's rule over the Palestinians, models that help explain various aspects of the status quo, not only the element of military coercion but also the intercommunal interactions.

"More than in any other war, including the Lebanon war, the Intifada led to a sense of frustration in the Israeli army," say Ze'ev Schiff and Ehud Ya'ari. "There are different reasons for this feeling. One of them is the knowledge that it is unable to make use of its might in the new form of warfare—civil insurrection. This was also the feeling at the end of the war in Lebanon. But this time, in the Intifada, it is more salient than in previous wars, because this time unarmed civilians are facing off against the best-equipped army in the Middle East. . . . If the superpowers learned this lesson bloodily [in Vietnam and Afghanistan], it is important that the army of a small nation that must conserve its strength not ignore it. It is certainly preferable to the intoxication with power that possessed the Israeli army after the Six-Day War" (Schiff and Ya'ari, *Intifada* [Jerusalem

and Tel Aviv: Shocken Publishing House, 1990]; in Hebrew).
The Intifada is, then, the "third front." This front is one facing
"a civilian uprising." "The Intifada was a war of a new type,"
Schiff and Ya'ari conclude.

A violent confrontation between communities is not a war, so
the comparison between the Intifada and "all other wars" or "the
previous wars" that Israel has undergone is invalid from the start.
True, in every war, as in the Intifada, the army is sent out to provide a military solution, but that is the only similarity. In a civilian uprising, as opposed to a conventional war, there is no front
line and the occupation of territory has no meaning. In the confrontation between communities, it is not the army that is on the
battlefield—it is every single individual in the community, without distinction between soldier and civilian. The confrontation
is not necessarily a violent encounter. It finds expression in all
spheres of life and activity, even in those of a civilian nature. In a
conventional war, the army defends the country's borders, while
in an intercommunal conflict it defends the regime. A conventional war lasts until one side wins, or until both sides tire and
everyone goes home. Intercommunal conflicts are chronic,
endemic, organic, and endless. They just go on and on. Intercommunal conflicts are twilight wars, in which every person (soldiers included) must swing between the concept that the other is
the enemy who must be destroyed and the concept that he is a
living, breathing human being. In a conventional war, the army
faces the enemy's conventional forces. In intercommunal conflicts, it faces civilians, but civilians who see themselves as soldiers in every sense of the word. There is no need to be a soldier
at the front in order to feel that you are at war, and it is not necessary to wear a uniform to feel that you are a soldier. The fact

that one side is armed with firearms and the other with slings hardly makes the intercommunal conflict a new form of warfare. Not only does the superiority of arms not determine the result of the conflict—but the absence of arms actually gives the "civilian" side an advantage. In a communal conflict—as opposed to a conventional war, in which victory is measured by the destruction of the enemy as a fighting force—victory is gauged by the collapse of the regime's base of support, in successfully influencing public opinion. A conventional war that is won ends, sooner or later, in a political settlement. An intercommunal conflict ends only after the opponents find a way of accepting one another at the deepest, metapolitical levels of their existence, after they have clarified questions of self-identity and legitimacy for themselves and to their neighbors.

One can claim that the Intifada has proven the need for a political solution, and that it has proven those generals who have repeatedly said that the Intifada has no military solution, only a political one, correct. But this is simplistic and does not assist in understanding the problem, much less in finding a solution. From the comparison of "Makarios and Bourguiba, Jomo Kenyata and Nkrumah" with Palestinian leaders, one understands the fallacy of using the colonial model to explain the Intifada and the Jewish-Arab conflict. The British and the French, "who negotiated with those they threw into jail," like Kenyata and Bourguiba, dismantled their colonial regimes and went home; the Israelis must negotiate with leaders who share their land. Chief of Staff Dan Shomron best pinpointed the difference: "I think of the future, with whom we will live here"—with the emphasis on the "here."

The Intifada is the fourth outbreak of the Jewish-Palestinian intercommunal conflict. The first two outbreaks, in the middle (1936) and at the end (1947–48) of the Mandatory period, were classic intercommunal struggles, in which the two groups fought under relatively equal conditions—both of them having to rely on illegal militias, and both lacking the advantages that control of a government confers. During the years of partition, 1949–67—and, in fact, until the 1970s—the Israeli-Arab conflict was one between states, meaning that it took the form of conventional warfare (1948–49, 1956, 1967, 1973). Yet the intercommunal confrontation continued, carried on by infiltrators, fedayeen, terrorist acts in Israel and elsewhere, and demonstrations and confrontations in the occupied territories.

In 1982, Israel launched a war in Lebanon that targeted both the PLO's military potential and the powerful base of Palestinian nationalism that had arisen in Beirut. Its perpetrators, Menachem Begin and Ariel Sharon, saw this as "a war for the Land of Israel." The aim was to destroy the independent power base of Palestinian nationalism in Lebanon, and thus to deal a final blow to Palestinian resistance on the West Bank and in Gaza. Begin and Sharon attached greater importance to the destruction of the Palestinians' "alternate homeland" than to the establishment of a "new order" in Lebanon. "If we win," said Rafael Eitan, then the Israeli chief of staff, "the struggle for the Land of Israel will look different." And, in fact, there is a direct link between the result of the third intercommunal confrontation in Lebanon and the outbreak of the fourth confrontation—the Intifada. The eviction of the PLO from Lebanon and its dispersion throughout the Arab world put an end to the Palestinian "armed struggle" option, an end to the dream that it would be possible to defeat Israel with terror, guerrilla warfare, or even conventional warfare. From

1982 onward, violent demonstrations and disturbances in the territories grew sixfold. There was a significant change in the relation between spontaneous disturbances and premeditated terrorist attacks—in 1984 there was one terrorist act for every eleven disturbances, while in 1987 there was one terrorist act for every eighteen disturbances. Sixty percent of the attacks involving firearms were local initiatives, rather than the execution of orders from PLO headquarters outside the country.

There has been a fundamental difference between Labor and Likud on the definition of the Israeli-Arab conflict. Labor has adhered to the view that with the establishment of Israel, the intercommunal conflict in Mandatory Palestine was transformed into a conflict between states. This view has not altered since the 1967 war and the occupation of the West Bank and Gaza. Likud, under the influence of Menachem Begin, has tended to emphasize the intercommunal aspects of the conflict and viewed the struggle for Greater Israel as its core.

Up until the end of the 1970s, the question of whether the conflict was one between states or between communities was not merely a theoretical one asked by historians after the fact. The opposing positions were guidelines for action, since actions, and blunders, could still determine what character the conflict would assume and therefore indicate how to resolve it. For example, had the Labor party proceeded with the "Jordanian option" (an interstate approach) in 1974 and given King Hussein a real foothold on the West Bank (as Henry Kissinger proposed), the internalization of the conflict, and its transformation into an intercommunal confrontation, would have been forestalled. But this did not happen, and three years later Menachem Begin was able to implement his policy, which he did with great tenacity.

The Camp David accords, the peace treaty with Egypt, the Lebanon war, the steps toward de facto annexation and distancing Jordan from a position of influence on the West Bank, were all stages in the transformation of the conflict into intercommunal strife.

Among the Arabs, as among the Israelis, there were also differing approaches, but they were expressed in other terms. On the Arab side, the dispute was between those who saw Israel as a pan-Arab problem (an interstate dispute) and those who saw it as a Palestinian problem. Israel's actions and those of the Arabs fed one another, and this led to a correlation between them. Both led to a Palestinization of the conflict. Not only did the struggle become intercommunal at the end of the Lebanon war; its focus shifted to within the former borders of Mandatory Palestine.

Even the PLO, which perceived the conflict as an Israeli-Palestinian dispute, did not understand that in its new phase, it was returning to its original territorial bounds—and that, as a result, it would be the Palestinians "inside" who would dictate its dynamics. Arguably, the PLO leadership failed to perceive revolutionary potential building up in the occupied territories, but a rational analysis of the power relationship between Israel and the Palestinians might also have led to the conclusion that the Palestinians would be worse off after the Intifada than they were before it. In any case, not only did the PLO not initiate the Intifada—although it tried to take credit for this in retrospect—but a long time went by before the PLO even knew what it all meant.

The Labor party (and the Israeli defense establishment, which continued to act in accordance with the interstate model) did not understand the significance of the Intifada either. The fundamental difference between Labor and the Likud on the essence of the conflict therefore continued, as though the issue had not already been decided, and when historians (including this author) defined the conflict as intercommunal, people automatically thought that they were Likud supporters!

The Intifada broke out with the maturation of the complex political, social, economic, and cultural processes that slowly transformed the Jewish Israeli nation-state and made it into a de facto binational state. In this sense, December 9, 1987, was the day when the intercommunal conflict was symbolically declared. More than being an event like the day a war breaks out, it was one in which reality broke, thundering, through the conceptual barrier. The moment the violent conflict erupted in its full magnitude, a new chapter in the history of the Jewish-Arab conflict began. Despite the fact that the Intifada was the fourth outbreak of this old conflict, it was unique in that it was the first general uprising against a Jewish Israeli regime.

The Intifada's declared goal was to put an end to the political-military status quo that had come into being in Palestine, and to the Jewish Israeli monopoly on public and governmental resources. Paradoxically, however, the Intifada could break out only because this status quo had become institutionalized and had created strong political, societal, economic, and cultural interactions between the Israelis and the Palestinians.

The type of relations created between the contending communities might be called "intimate enmity." There are those who believe that confrontational and hostile relations can create only alienation and separation. They ignore the fact that confrontation creates intercommunal interactions that are sometimes stronger than peaceful relations. Obviously, these interactions are of a negative character. They bear a huge emotional and political burden, however, which shapes both the character of intercommunal relations and relations within the communities. It is impossible to understand the Intifada without following the tangential circles in which Palestinians and Israelis have moved during twenty years of Israeli rule. The most important of these circles is, of course, the system of coercion imposed by the Israelis. The military government rested largely on deterrents: "The display of force is preferable to the use of force" has been its motto. As long as the Palestinians were still dazed by the occupation and feared that the Israelis would do to them what they would do to the Israelis were their positions reversed, the military administration could coerce and use force in a controlled fashion. The regime was able to operate at a low economic and military cost; as a result, it was given tight budgets and relatively inferior manpower.

The use of various manipulative methods ("the carrot and the stick"), creating conflicts between various sectors of the population, and the absolute arbitrariness of the regime, brought about the corruption of both the conqueror and the conquered. The better acquainted the Palestinians became with the Israeli regime and its weaknesses, the further the military government's power to deter declined—and deterrence, as noted, was the foundation of its doctrine of control. Every imposed regime creates friction and bitterness and humiliates those it rules over. The Israeli military government was not, however, just a "foreign regime" devoted to frustrating attempts to rebel against it. The tension between the occupier and the occupied derived from more than just the lack of freedom and punitive actions. The military regime was from the start a means of imposing the communal interests of the Jewish group. It served the Jewish community as a tool for dispossessing the Palestinian community of its collective assets.

The policy of Israeli governments (whether directly applied or in the guise of military government orders) and its implementation made it clear to the Palestinians not only that their freedom had been taken from them, but also that their very existence as a national community was threatened. The expropriation of half the land on the West Bank, the commandeering of water sources, the subordination of the economy to the needs of the Jewish collective, discrimination in commerce and labor, the settlements, obstacles to infrastructural development, the systematic deportation of Palestinian leaders, the closing of universities, the censorship—all these aroused deep apprehension about the chances of surviving as a Palestinian collective under Israeli rule.

The survival of the collective occupied the Palestinian elite, but the dispossession of the community had a direct effect on the life of every Palestinian individual. Discrimination in the economic system made almost a third of all Palestinian wage earners into "hewers of wood and drawers of water" for the Jewish collective. Many worked under humiliating conditions, liable at any time to have their honor affronted. They were the victims of attitudes formed of preconceptions and stereotypes, and the targets of insults with more than a whiff of racism. Many feared that they had lost control of their personal destiny, and that their remaining self-respect was fast running out.

Deep concern about the fate of the collective, combined with the lack of personal security, brought the Palestinian community as a whole to assess its plight, infusing it with ideology. This was the transition from the stage of acquiescence to the stage of revolt. Paradoxically, the feelings of anger and the willingness to rebel against the status quo increased precisely because, by all objective standards, the Palestinian community's socioeconomic position had improved. Most Palestinians' standard of living and level of education rose dramatically, yet this merely heightened the sense of being discriminated against. It is, after all, relative rather than absolute deprivation that causes intercommunal tension. The Palestinians did not compare their objective condition after twenty years of occupation to their situation before the occupation, but rather to that of the Jewish population. One of the notable consequences of the intimate interaction between the two societies was that the Palestinians began to see the Jewish population as their reference group.

The Palestinians had observed the swift rise in the Jewish community's standard of living and the establishment of an Israeli consumer society. They were also intimately acquainted with both the strengths and the weaknesses of Israel's political system. The Israelis, they knew, considered themselves a morally sensitive, humanist democratic-liberal society, and they scrupulously guarded their national consensus. Familiarity with the Jewish Israeli system accordingly gave the Palestinians a sense that launching a violent rebellion would not be catastrophic for them, because the Israelis would never dare use all the power at their disposal with the necessary ruthlessness.

The uprising of December 1987 thus had both rational and irrational foundations. There can be no doubt that it broke out spontaneously, without any actual preparation or calculated planning by the Palestinian elite. It was an unplanned eruption of all the political, economic, and social pressures that had built up during twenty years of occupation. In retrospect, it is possible to analyze the causes one by one and set out the Intifada's political goals, but this is a rationalization of an event that, according to all testimony, was not premeditated—an event lacking a defined political or military plan.

The Israeli defense establishment can be criticized for being taken by surprise and ridiculed for not having read the writing on the wall. Masters of hindsight emphasize "the deep background of the uprising [and] the national-economic-social powder keg that was going to explode in any case." Such criticism implies that the Intifada could have been averted had the defense establishment frustrated the efforts of the Jewish Israeli community to despoil the Palestinian collective and create a dual, hierarchical society, which created the "powder keg." In short, one would have to return to the seventh day of the Six-Day War and start again, if that were humanly possible—or to be less cynical— to recognize the inevitability of the Intifada, given the "national-economic-social" conditions created since the occupation.

The outbreak of the Intifada was not an event; rather, it was the culmination of a process. The Israelis determined the arena and the rules of the game. Those who consciously chose to transform the interstate conflict into an intercommunal one should have anticipated that the threatened community would respond to the challenge. The Israelis erred in refusing to see the Palestinians as a community, and as a result could not believe that they were capable of responding as a community. The roots of this error lie in the ethnocentric Jewish worldview—the inability to recognize the existence of another legitimate collective between the Jordan and the sea. As a result, when the Intifada broke out, Israelis internalized only its violent aspect. They grasped only the confrontation between the Palestinians and the authorities, and were completely blind to its other components: community mobilization, the attempts to create an independent economic and social infrastructure, and especially the significance of the mobilization of the Palestinian masses in the conflict.

This irrational attitude, in which there is a refusal to comprehend the link between cause and effect, is what has made the Intifada mushroom into a "war"—that is, a threat to the very existence of the Jewish collective. The process is well known from other divided societies; in his book *Ethnopolitics* (New York: Columbia University Press, 1981) Joseph Rothschild has put it as follows: "Once a specific confrontational situation has been perceived and defined in a particular manner by one of the parties—be it dominant or subordinate—this generates strong pressures for the other side to respond in mirror image terms. A kind of antagonistic collusion may even set in between them—to prevent alternative perspectives from emerging and to facilitate their respective mobilizations and enforcement of ethno-political solidarity" (p. 131). The spontaneous popular Palestinian revolt, expressed in physical and verbal violence, awakened spontaneous popular responses among the Jewish population that were no less extreme.

The Intifada has, then, increased mutual hostility and polarization, and has thus decreased the chances of a dialogue. This polarization was expressed in opinion polls, in the voting booths, and right there on the battleground of the streets: the regime shed its remaining pretensions to a "benign occupation" and imposed unrestricted bureaucratic violence, aimed at humiliating the Palestinians and proving who was mightier. Dehumanization and brutalization have become commonplace in the security forces, who have magnified the feelings of animosity among the Palestinians and their willingness to take risks, creating a sense that sooner or later there will be a horrible bloodbath. The Palestinians' boldness, the widespread use of firearms to disperse demonstrations, and a radical change in the army's rules of engagement have steadily increased the number of casualties. Yet largely to the credit of the military authorities, who—although accused of weakness by the right and of cruelty by the left—have held consistently to a policy of controlled use of firepower, there has been no bloodbath.

There can be no doubt that had the army made use of all the means at its disposal, the Intifada would have been drowned in Palestinian blood. But the unrestricted use of firearms is not legitimate in a society that links itself with the Western liberal world. Even more important, perhaps, the escalation of coercion would have created fissures in the Israeli national consensus—might even have ended it. As one Israeli general said: "There are things that you don't do in a society like ours. If you do them, you will divide the people."

Arabs outside Israel have seen the restrictions imposed on themselves by the Israeli military authorities as part of a conspiracy to perpetuate the current situation. "The Likud is interested in the perpetuation of the Intifada, in order to destroy the Jordanian option and afterwards to bring about a population transfer," one Jordanian said. These Arabs found it difficult to understand why the Israeli army was not reacting as the Jordanian and Syrian armies had reacted in similar situations—with tank shelling and machine-gun fire.

The Palestinians knew the Israelis, however, and were conscious of their sensitivity. They grasped very well that they must not provoke them intolerably by using firearms (although they had only limited quantities of such weapons). They also knew that terrorist attacks on Jewish citizens would increase the solidarity of the Jewish collective, and so harm the Palestinians themselves. As a result, they confined their violent acts to throwing stones and Molotov cocktails, and to the use of "cold" weapons like axes and knives. They understood that the better part of their power lay in the mass mobilization of unarmed demonstrators to clash with and provoke the security forces. In this way, when the soldiers lost control, the Palestinians could present their wounded as helpless victims.

Despite its hundreds of dead and thousands of wounded, the Intifada thus remained confined to a framework of controlled violence. As in all intercommunal conflicts, the intensity of the violent confrontation was relatively low, because an intercommunal conflict is by nature complex and political rather than unambiguous and military. A chronic disease is not cured by radical surgery. The real campaign did not take place in the city streets, between young men with their faces masked and other young men in Israel Defence Forces uniforms. It took place on the television screens. Rather than on military control, it centered on public opinion.

The Intifada, let it be reiterated, was a spontaneous uprising that broke out without any rational computation of profit and loss, opportunities and risks. But once it had broken out, Palestinian leaders began weighing the options rationally—how best to use it to advance the Palestinian interest. The first reactions from the outside world indicated that the civil uprising could be made into a valuable political tool by exploiting sympathetic public opinion. The unpleasant spectacle of defenseless civilians being beaten, wounded, and killed by an army armed to the teeth were seen on television screens all over the world and created empathy for the Palestinian cause. The emotional effect was doubled and redoubled because this time it was Jews who were the oppressive power. The image of the quintessential oppressed people metamorphosed into oppressors was dramatic and could leave no viewer apathetic. The Palestinians understood that from this point of view, they were lucky that it was Jews who were oppressing them. Who would have paid any attention to them had the Turks or the Iranians conquered their land?

For a long time, the Palestinians believed that sympathetic world public opinion would produce political results, and the Israelis indeed found themselves in a delicate and inferior political position. Condemnation followed condemnation, and even the United States, their main source of support, felt itself obliged to take account of public opinion and establish a political link with the PLO. But the Palestinians' rational considerations and their successful implementation were based on an erroneous approach. They believed that world opinion and the positions taken by Western governments would create effective pressure on Israel, which would be forced to withdraw from the territories. This indirect approach contained a strong echo of their old perception—that Israeli was nothing more than an agent of Western imperialism, an object rather than a subject. They believed that the Israelis could not exist without massive support from the West, and that when this was removed, Israel would collapse like a giant with straw legs.

The Palestinians have never understood the nature of the relations between the Jewish state and the Western world, and the psychological scar left by thousands of years of intimate interaction between the Jewish people and their Christian persecutors.

The strong emotional response to the sight of the oppressed turned oppressor should actually have made it clear to them that the Western world perceived the Intifada through the prism of Jewish-Christian relations, and not in the context of Israeli oppression of the Palestinians. It was not so much the suffering of the Palestinians that influenced Western reactions as the relief many felt at seeing the oppressed Jews inflicting pain on others, thus forfeiting their moral superiority. Yet the Palestinians remained totally alien to this convoluted, tragic Jewish-gentile dichotomy. There was no chance that the West would exert effective political pressure capable of dislodging the Israelis. Moreover, the Israelis summoned up their ancient defense mechanism, the one that labels all foreign criticism and condemnation of Israel as anti-Semitism. When the Palestinians realized their mistake, at the end of the Intifada's second year, they made a rational decision—to change direction. World opinion would not affect the status quo, they understood. That would change only via a spontaneous Israeli decision to do so.

Bringing Israel to the point where it could make a unilateral decision required an attempt to shatter the solidarity of the Israeli political center by wearing away the legitimacy that the Jewish collective gave to its government. The Palestinians believed the biased political analysis of their supporters on the Israeli left. One "dove" composed the following estimation: "The paradox of the weakness of power [is]: the more the regime bases itself on the use of brutal force, the more it exhausts the resources of its power and strengthens the opposition of the oppressed. This is the meaning of the sudden collapse of dictatorial police states . . . that have collapsed like houses of cards. The growing and persistent determination of the Palestinians is deepening and widening fissures [in Israeli solidarity]. . . . The cost of the occupation is penetrating ever deeper into the consciousness of Israeli society." He and others like him did not discern the great difference between "authority," or legitimacy, which underlies the regimes of divided societies, and "dictatorial police states." In divided societies, the regime seeks only the legitimacy of the community that granted it its authority. It does not ask for legitimacy from the subject collective, because the subject collective is hostile. Every attempt by the subjugated ethnic group to challenge the regime's legitimacy increases the cohesiveness of the ruling collective and consolidates its support for the regime.

The Palestinians and their sympathizers on the Israeli left wished to draw similarities between the Intifada and the collapse of the Eastern European dictatorships in the face of popular uprisings. But this comparison was baseless, and in fact the cohesiveness of the Israeli political center has not eroded. The unexpected uprising produced great consternation, penetrating questions, and stormy debates, but its actual influence was largely on the margins of the political spectrum. Left-wing groups calling for an end to the occupation proliferated, and right-wing groups calling for the "transfer" (deportation) of the Arab population grew more popular, but elections at the height of the Intifada (in 1988) brought about no real change in the division of the Knesset between the two parties representing the Israeli center—the Likud (center-right) and Labor (center-left).

It may be that the real test of the Intifada's effect on the Jewish public was the phenomenon of conscientious objection by soldiers refusing to serve in the territories. Among the hundreds of thousands of regular and reserve soldiers who have served in

in de facto control of "liberated areas"—villages the security forces did not enter.

The Intifada's leaflets called this effort "the replacement of the existing regime with national rule." This voluntary system focused the attention of the media and made a major impression. "A dual regime has been created in the territories—the Israeli military administration and the shadow administration of the popular committees," concluded Schiff and Ya'ari, "two administrations that not only provide services and aid—each in its own way and according to its ability—but also frequently take punitive and retributive measures. The Palestinians consolidated a kind of low-level, crude autonomy, and stopped there."

But the reality was less heroic than the image. The Palestinians were unable to establish an independent physical and economic infrastructure that would allow them to sever their connections with the Israeli system, which had long since swallowed the West Bank and Gaza Strip. The Palestinians could play at growing vegetables and rabbits in their backyards or at boycotting Israeli products for which there were alternatives (cigarettes, certain food products). They could stage partial commercial strikes and organize parades through "liberated villages" in front of television cameras, but their real situation became clear when the Israelis decided to take extreme measures. When the supply of gasoline was halted, when telephone and electric lines were cut, when they were forbidden to export and the supply of vegetables to their wholesale markets was disrupted, the Palestinians fell back to a very "crude autonomy" indeed—the autonomy of a prison. The Israeli military administration stopped pretending to "supply services and assistance" and became no more than a punitive operation. The inevitable result was a 30–40 percent decline in the standard of living, a dramatic decline in economic activity, bitterness, and frustration.

What was important to the Palestinians was not the objective result of the establishment of communal institutions or the fruits of the effort to establish an independent infrastructure. It was the fact that they could mobilize the will of their community, a will that did not diminish in adversity. Many of them were acquainted with the history of the Zionist movement, and—how ironic—found historical parallels with the rival national liberation movement. The Palestinians understood the historic lesson the Zionist movement had learned—that subjective will can overcome objective reality if the resources of the entire community are mobilized, if proto-sovereign institutions are established on the basis of voluntary association, and if a pragmatic policy unhampered by absolutist ideologies is pursued. In fact, some of the practical and even symbolic steps they took gave the impression that they had studied their Zionist textbooks diligently.

It may well be that the establishment of "local authority" was a convergent response to a challenge similar to the one faced by the Zionist movement under British rule, and that this is the source of the similarity between it and the institutions of the "state-to-be" of the Jewish community in Mandatory Palestine. But then how to explain the use of the Exodus symbol, the ship the Palestinians planned to sail to Israel's shores at the height of the Intifada, imitating the famous refugee boat of 1946? And how can one not notice in the Palestinian declaration of independence entire sentences lifted from its Israeli counterpart? Or the fundamental significance attached to the U.N. partition resolution of 1947 as a basis for the legitimacy of the Palestinian state?

Israel's drastic response to these Palestinian actions shows that it, at least, feared that the Palestinians had mastered the material.

The Palestinians succeeded in conducting a relatively controlled confrontation, based on realistic considerations. The leaders of the uprising did not permit any departure from a fairly rigid framework of disobedience, one that continually took into account the populace's endurance. Their realism was, however, expressed primarily in the political sphere. They sent the PLO in Tunis and its leader, Yassir Arafat, a clear message: the uprising must be translated into a political program grounded in reality. The illusion that Israel did not exist, because the Palestinians could not accept its existence, and the belief that Israel could be wished away, they said, would lead to catastrophe. Ignoring the real balance of power, the local Palestinians warned, would also mean the end of what little could still be saved.

This was the background to the Palestinian declaration of independence in November 1988, which recognized the partition of Palestine, and therefore the State of Israel—although unfortunately some forty years too late. The declaration and the willingness of the Palestinians to compromise would once have been historic events of the utmost importance; three years into the Intifada, however, they were simply incidents drowned in the torrent of events. Another historic development that was a direct outcome of the Intifada was the declaration severing Jordan from the territories. King Hussein understood the meaning of the uprising and concluded that there was no possible way to return to the status quo ante of "the unity of the two banks." He understood that the Jewish-Palestinian intercommunal struggle was irreversible. Wishing to prevent the spread of this conflict east of the Jordan, he decided to renounce his claims to the West Bank.

In doing so, of course, Hussein dispersed the mirage called "the Jordanian option," which had allowed the Labor party to sidestep the intercommunal character of the conflict. Yet no other proposal replaced it. The Likud mocked the Labor leaders, whose program had evaporated, but was itself unable to formulate a positive policy, other than continued rule over the rebellious population by force. In 1989, when the Likud leadership was prodded into "coming up with something," it announced an "elections plan," which, like the autonomy plan that had preceded it, basically accepted that an intercommunal conflict was going on. This plan was at the time considered "historic" and a "basis for the peace process." Yet its authors' evasions, and the hurdles they put in the way of its implementation, proved that they were ideologically unable to contend with the existence of a Palestinian collective. They sought to occupy themselves with the technicalities of the proposed elections in order to evade the decisive question—the size and composition of the constituency involved, or, in other words, who belonged to the collective that was being given the opportunity to vote. Had they been willing to recognize the Palestinian collective, they would not, of course, have needed to occupy themselves with the method by which its representatives would be chosen. The difficulties they placed in the way of negotiations derived from a desire to present a plan that would be unacceptable to the other side. In any case, the "elections plan" was added to the pile of papers stamped with the initials OBE—overtaken by events.

The political change brought about by the Intifada, both on the political and the conceptual level, is not the sum total of the social and cultural transmutation that the Palestinian community has undergone. The popular struggle, the dead, the suffering and grief, the elation and the despair, the mutual aid, and the readiness to cope with the difficulties of day-to-day living, month after month, year after year—all these forged the Palestinian community. The Intifada, like every other profound collective experience, was a unique spiritual event for those who lived through it, one that could not be comprehended in full from the outside. Like every other profound collective experience, it almost immediately produced cultural expressions of its emotional intensity. Hundreds of poems, stories, plays, graffiti, and books were written, drawn, taped, and orally recounted. The Israeli censor's attempts to gag the Palestinians were pathetic. A joke, story of heroism, or poem would be born in a detention camp, and within a day or two it would have spread throughout the territories—which was not surprising in a society with a well-developed tradition of oral communication.

The Intifada and the sacrifices of the people in the territories also sparked the imaginations and awakened the pride of Palestinians outside the territories, and of the entire Arab world. But the literary compositions of Arab writers and poets elsewhere, including those of Palestinians scattered around the world, were necessarily at second hand. In the territories themselves, no one was writing passionate lyrics; there they were composing popular revolutionary songs aimed at mobilizing the community for the struggle, imbuing it with hope and sustaining its spirit with macabre humor.

The Intifada caused profound social changes, creating extensive social mobility and, in particular, thoroughly challenging the traditional patriarchal social hierarchy. This challenge found expression in the rebellion of young men and women—those born into the Israeli occupation—against their parents, and against the norms and values of the older generation. The Intifada revealed the strengths of the Palestinian community in the occupied territories, which had grown away from the larger body of the Palestinian people, but also its weaknesses—especially the fact that its primitive instincts were easily aroused, that it tended to be swept away by irrational urges, lacked civic culture, could not control internal violence, had difficulty sticking to realistic objectives, and felt a deep inferiority to, and helpless anger against, the West and its hated agent, Zionism.

The unique experience of the Palestinian community in the territories during more than a quarter of a century of Israeli occupation, and especially in the Intifada, has created its own political, social, and cultural motifs. Nonetheless, the link between it and the Palestinian nation outside the territories has not been, and cannot be, severed. One cannot reasonably expect that families torn apart arbitrarily will remain so, or that geopolitical circumstances will be sufficient to sunder a national tradition or unmake political solidarity. On the other hand, Palestinians who have not interacted intimately with Israeli society, who have not lived under Israeli rule, and who have not risen up against it, were not party to a collective experience that has produced unmistakable marks of identification. An ethnic subgroup that might be called the "1967 Arabs" has been created, like the "1948 Arabs"—the Palestinian community under Israeli rule from 1948. This differentiation from the Palestinians outside the territories has been a long and complex process, and will continue if the geopolitical status quo is not altered. The unification of the Palestinian nation on both sides of the Green Line separating the territories from pre-1967 Israel has, in contrast, already been accomplished.

Numerous scholars and politicians have, since 1967, dealt with the relationship between the Arabs of Israel and the Arabs of the territories. Since December 1987 there has been a sharp public debate in Israel over the question of whether the Intifada has crossed the Green Line. As one might expect, the issue is perceived less from a scholarly-empirical perspective than from a political-ideological one. Furthermore, even the scholars who have produced statistical tables and studies have not been without political opinions, and based on their attitudes to the future of the territories, they have reached widely differing conclusions (often from the selfsame data).

In general, those who argue that the Intifada has indeed crossed the Green Line believe that the line has been erased and see the Arabs of Israel and the Arabs of the territories as partners in a campaign against Israel. In support of their conclusion, they cite data on the dramatic increase in terrorist attacks within the Green Line. According to published data, the number of terrorist acts within the Green Line increased by 250 percent in the period 1987–89, and the number of "nationalist acts" by 400 percent. Acts of nonviolent civil disobedience (such as raising Palestinian flags and defacing Israeli national symbols) increased from 150 per year in 1987 to 1,000 in 1989. Over the course of the Intifada, Israeli Arabs have staged general strikes no fewer than nine times.

The polarization of Israeli Arabs' political positions has been expressed in elections to the Knesset. In 1984, 51 percent voted for non-Zionist Arab parties, but in 1988 this rose to 59 percent. (This trend was reversed in the 1992 election, as described in Chapter 5.) In the 1988 municipal elections, the number of Arab mayors affiliated with Zionist parties declined steeply. The Committee of Arab Mayors and the Arab Higher Coordinating Committee increased their strength. They guided, supervised, and coordinated many political initiatives and became the representative organs of the Israeli Arab minority. Among other things, they supplied financial aid to the Palestinian struggle.

At the same time, the leaders of the Arab community emphasized that they did not support copying the methods of struggle used in the territories inside Israel. "You should distinguish between players and fans," one of their leaders said. "We're fans." The leadership sharply condemned terrorist and subversive acts and exerted great effort to preserve order during demonstrations and general strikes. This deliberate effort to channel Palestinians' solidarity and anger against Israeli repression into nonviolence did not satisfy the advocates of a hard-line policy, who argued that the Intifada is nothing but a catalyst in an ongoing process of Palestinization, pressure for autonomy, and separation from Israel—a new and dangerous situation. Ariel Sharon accused the Israeli Arabs of having made common cause with the enemy, saying they wished "to destroy us instead of fighting together with us, as loyal citizens of the state."

These harsh opinions about the Intifada's incursion into "little Israel" and the political polarization of Israeli Arabs hid a deeper fear that Israeli Arabs would no longer be content to fight for individual rights and would consolidate into a united national minority demanding recognition of its collective rights. The change of Arab voting patterns in Knesset elections, the establishment of independent Arab parties, the decision to establish a united slate of Arab candidates for elections to the Histadrut trade union (1989), and the development of independent communal and cultural institutions funded by overseas Arab foundations emphasized the fact that even "little Israel" would not escape an intercommunal conflict.

The Israeli Arabs' weapons in this battle were not violence and civil disobedience; they were votes. In the 1988 Knesset elections, the turnout of Arab voters grew significantly. Had they all voted for Arab parties, fourteen Arabs would have been serving in the Knesset. The Arabs' ability to exploit their hold on the balance of power between the two large political blocs was evident in the elections to institutions of the Center for Local Government, the national mayors' conference. They threw their votes to the Likud, giving that party's candidate for the chair of the Center for Local Government his majority. This proved that the Israeli Arab leadership could approach politics pragmatically without being tied down by simplistic ideology. This approach became clearer in the 1992 Knesset election (see Chapter 5).

The government took several measures to retard the consolidation of a united Israeli Arab collective. First, it warned the Israeli Arabs against dreaming of national autonomy, educational autonomy, and independent institutions "that would cut them off from the central flow of life in the country." Second, it pronounced that the polarization was the result of explicit instructions from the PLO and was nothing more than a "division of labor" between the Arabs in Israel and the Arabs in the territories—the Israeli Arabs being charged with destroying Israel from within, while the Arabs in the territories attacked from outside. There were repeated attempts to force upon Israeli Arabs the "choice" between loyalty to the State of Israel as the Jewish state and loyalty to Palestinian national goals. Attempts to disqualify Arab slates of candidates on the basis of their platforms failed, but the Knesset passed a law prohibiting the receipt of funds from "hostile organizations." The use of drastic measures to suppress legal political activity contradicts the image of Israel as a liberal democracy, so right-wing groups stressed the acts of violence committed within "little Israel" and Israeli Arab leaders' vocal support of the Intifada and the PLO. If it is possible to construct a conspiracy theory and rouse fears of "a fire that will spread to the Palestinian population in Israel," it is possible to call for the declaration of a state of emergency that will suspend the civil rights of Israeli Arabs.

Just as it was important for right-wing groups to highlight the Palestinization of the Arabs of Israel and the Intifada's incursion across the Green Line, so it was important for the supporters of territorial compromise to prove that the reverse was true. In their opinion, the Intifada actually "strengthened the Green Line and emphasized the differences between the Palestinian Arabs who are citizens of Israel and their brothers in the territories." The Haifa University researcher Sami Smooha categorically rejected the conclusion that the Arabs in Israel and in the territories have become a single ethnic group. "The Intifada was a timely reminder that the Green Line is as solid as it ever was," he asserted. The Israeli Arabs did not join in the Intifada because, unlike their brothers across the Green Line, they do not have to endure an occupation regime, do not aspire to liberation, and can conduct a democratic struggle.

To justify their position, left-wing groups minimized the importance of acts of violence by Israeli Arabs, pointing to the higher turnout by Arab voters as proof of their desire to become fully integrated into Israeli political life. The general strikes, they said, were an internal Israeli Arab matter. They have produced studies showing that the Israeli element in Israeli Arab identity has grown stronger, although they admit that "the Intifada has also brought about a strengthening of the Palestinian element." There is no contradiction, they argue, between these two components of their identity. Israeli Arabs support the establishment of a Palestinian state in the occupied territories, but their own struggle is perceived as an effort to "advance their interests within the State of Israel, like other groups within the Jewish population." For this reason, Israeli Arabs underscore their cooperation with the Jewish left against the annexation of the territories and against the rising power of the right. According to this analysis, the ideological bond uniting the Jewish left and the Israeli Arabs is stronger than the ethnic bond that unites the latter with the Arabs of the territories. Yet studies of ethnic groups indicate that this argument is baseless. "Ethnicity," Joseph Rothschild writes, "has one advantage over other modes of personal identity and of social linkage, namely its capacity to arouse and engage the most intense, deep and private emotional sentiments." He adds: "Once activated, ethnic identity, ethnic interest and especially ethnic anxiety tend to neutralize and to subsume emotionally more abstract commitments to functional social groups" (pp. 60–61). The disintegration of a united Jewish-Arab party, the Progressive List for Peace, into its ethnic components (despite the strong ideological bond) proved that this rule applies to the Israeli Arabs too, and testified to the weakness of the ideological ties between them and the Jewish left.

Yet this conclusion, which leads to the elimination of the geographic fault line and to the establishment of an ethnic fault throughout the entire area west of the Jordan, is inconsistent with the ideological desire to preserve, at all costs, the distinction between the territories (and their inhabitants) and Israel proper. By defining the link to their brothers in terms of "two states for two peoples" on the one hand and "the struggle for civil equality in Israel" on the other, one might well reach the conclusion that Israeli Arabs want to remain distinct from the Arabs of the territories. So long as only 7.5 percent of Israeli Arabs are interested in moving to a Palestinian state should one be established, and only 13.5 percent wish to see Israel disappear, so the argument runs, they cannot be considered an integral part of the Palestinian community in the territories. After all, everyone knows that the latter is a radical community that unanimously supports violence and rebellion and wishes to live in a Palestinian state. As long as Israeli Arabs do not rise up against the Israeli regime like their brothers—something they are not doing, and will not do, there would seem to be reason to adhere to the distinction between the two collectives. This also assures supporters of territorial compromise that the Green Line lives on. The fact that more than two-thirds of the Arabs in Israel define their identity in Palestinian terms, and that more than half of them support a "militant struggle for peace and equality," wins them the label "non-radical militants," but for some reason this is not sufficient as a test of their ethnic Palestinian identity.

There is more than a trace of paternalism and bias in defining the identity of Israeli Arabs according to an arbitrary test of political behavior and in accentuating the differences between them and the Arabs of the territories. The definition of Jewish Israeli identity is not cast in terms of political behavior. Would anyone dare divide the Jewish collective in terms of its "radicalization" or "moderation," and decide that Rabbi Kahane's followers or members of the left-wing Citizens' Rights Movement belong to a Jewish subgroup? Even attempts to determine the self-identity of communities by their citizenship status—that is, Israeli Arabs are Israeli citizens and Palestinians are not Israeli citizens—is insupportable. According to this test, the Palestinians on the West Bank are Jordanians, a definition no one dares use, because it is absurd.

The salient differences between the political behavior of Israeli Arabs and the Arabs of the territories and their forms of political mobilization derive from the manifest difference in their objective situation. Israeli Arabs have wisely developed their own models of political-communal activity, and in doing so have made sophisticated use of their status as equal citizens in the State of Israel. The level of political mobilization among Israeli Arabs reached a record high during the Intifada, as demonstrated by data on their support for general strikes (74 percent in 1988, as opposed to 61 percent in 1985) and for the Arab Mayors' Committee (71 percent in 1988, as opposed to 63 percent in 1985), and the especially high voter turnout for the 1988 Knesset elections. They will not play into the hands of the Jewish right and abandon the legitimate struggle in favor of violence and civil disobedience. Some wish to see in this political behavior a struggle for "equality and integration" distinguishing the Israeli Arabs from the Palestinians in the territories, who "aspire to separation and sovereignty." If they think that this somehow makes Israeli Arabs into a separate ethnic subgroup, they are engaging in wishful thinking.

At the end of the 1980s, the Palestinian community in the State of Israel (the "1948 Arabs") and the Palestinian community in the territories (the "1967 Arabs") reached an irreversible level of communal mobilization. They had passed the threshold at which their political mobilization became "highly resistant to being directed toward alternative perspectives." The challenges the two groups presented to the Jewish collective in demanding recognition as a national group were identical, although they adjusted their tactics to the prevailing conditions in Israel and the territories. On the ideological level, the challenge of the Israeli Arabs was much more acute than that presented by the Arabs of the territories. An external solution in the shape of territorial compromise, many Israelis believed, might be found for the Arabs of the territories. The Israeli Arabs' demands for recognition as a collective and for equal political rights raised unsolvable questions about the character of the State of Israel as the state of the Jewish people. Was this a liberal Western state with equal rights for all its citizens? On the practical level, the challenge of the Palestinians in the territories was more urgent, because they wished to destroy the status quo by force, while the Israeli Arabs were willing to pursue democratic means. The regime's reaction was proportional to the challenge, so in the territories coercion was applied, while within Israeli proper the authorities used manipulative methods.

The distinction between the demand to establish a Palestinian state and the recognition of the Israeli Arabs as a national minority is of great significance on the political level, but not on the metapolitical and symbolic levels. On both levels, the Jewish collective faces the necessity of either recognizing or not recognizing a symmetry of demands, and therefore also the relativity of rights. The Intifada has sharpened the interrelationship between the Palestinians' demands for a state in the territories and the Israeli Arabs' demands for recognition as a national minority. It has proven that these are two facets of a single question. Not only the spokesmen for the right—who have warned that every concession in the territories will bring about the amputation of Arab regions in Israel proper—testified to this; Israeli Arab intellectuals would agree. When it looked as if the Intifada were producing political fruit and there seemed to be a real possibility that the peace process would bring about the recognition of the political rights of the Arabs in the territories, Israeli Arabs began grappling with the question of their own fate. How could it be, they reflected, that the Arabs in the territories would get a state, or even autonomy, while the Arabs in Israel remained unrecognized as a collective?

In this context, ideas were raised about territorial, communal, or cultural autonomy within Israel. The issue was discussed only among Arab intellectuals and scholars. The Israeli Arab establishment opposed both the idea and any discussion of it. The major reason for this aversion was the well-founded fear that the debate would serve as an excuse for the authorities to take revenge on Arab bodies. Government Minister in Charge of Arab Affairs Ehud Olmert publicly warned: "I think that whoever talks about autonomy is talking about strengthening the infrastructure that must bring about the separation of the Arabs of Israel from the state. . . . That, in my opinion, is the reason that we must under no circumstances recognize the Arab Higher Coordinating Committee. The Committee is endeavoring to grant legitimacy to the idea of autonomy . . . and we will not cooperate with anyone connected with them."

The opposition to any institutionalized separatism on an ethnic basis (political or even cultural-educational autonomy) is common to all the Zionist political parties. Even left-wing Zionist groups consider Jewish-Arab cooperation a necessary condition for improving the personal and communal status of the

Israeli Arabs. Ethnic separatism, they believe, would be a sure recipe for perpetuating inequity and institutionalizing discrimination. The problem is, of course, that it was the Jews, not the Arabs, who created the existing institutionalized ethnic separation. The discrimination against Arabs, in all spheres, is based on manifestly ethnic criteria and is secured in the country's laws and the practices of its institutions. The Israelis who wish to cooperate with the Palestinians and who oppose their ethnic separatism do not propose to revoke ethnic separatism for Jews. On the contrary, most of them see inequality before the law, and the lack of freedom to define community affiliation according to any criterion other than the ethnic group one is born into, as positions consonant with liberal values. The preeminence of the Jewish collective, which they call "the Jewish state" is, after all, a supreme value for left-wing Zionism as well. Their support for the establishment of a Palestinian state in the territories is a way to resolve the contradiction between the principle of communal-civic equality and the institutional inequality of the Israeli Arab community. The national aspirations of the Israeli Arab minority "must be expressed in the future Palestinian state," not in Israel, because otherwise Israel will become "a binational state."

The creation of a Palestinian state and the recognition of Israeli Arabs as a national minority are, then, two aspects of the same issue in the eyes of both the Jewish right and the Zionist left. The Palestinian community on both sides of the Green Line is a single ethnic collective struggling with the Jewish collective on two fronts. One cannot rule out the possibility that the continuation of the geopolitical status quo will bring about the consolidation of Palestinian methods of struggle.

The Intifada sharpened all these ideological conundrums and

deeply rooted existential anxieties. It did not create new dilemmas—the dilemmas have not changed for seventy years. Neither did it solve any dilemma—no one has been able to shake free of the conventional answers and ask the pertinent questions. When the plot of the twenty-year occupation got inextricably tangled, the Israelis brought in a deus ex machina. The curtain fell on the status quo and its place was taken by the Intifada, the "last act," during which the longed-for catharsis had to arrive, finally. One thousand days later, when the plot again got inextricably tangled, the deus once more emerged from his machina.

CHAPTER FOUR

DEUS EX MACHINA

When a plot gets hopelessly tangled in classical Greek theater, a large box drops from the flies. From it emerges one of the gods. He ties up the loose ends, and the play, which has already gone on too long, reaches its anticipated denouement. Not that the dilemmas have been resolved or the ways of fate understood, but the audience can go home with its catharsis. After all, they were not looking for an answer, only for consolation. And tomorrow there will be another play.

Although the ancient Greeks may have invented the deus ex machina, it is perhaps the Semites who have developed this dramatic technique to supreme perfection. In the ongoing drama of the Israeli-Arab conflict, both the critics and the players have dispensed with plot. For them, history is nothing but an endless series of unexpected events. The god from the machine constantly intervenes to fake a resolution of the story's complications, one sufficient to allow the curtain to come down, or go up, as required. Pious hopes and towering fears are postponed to the next act, and so it goes on. The agonized audience, whose distress these rituals presume to express, does not dare question the tragedy's basic structure. It wants to forget the dissension and violence of the present, to fight off despair, to turn a blind eye to the ominous contradictions—and yearns to put off all its dreams and nightmares until tomorrow. Journalists and authors of political texts, commentators and thinkers, all gladly offer the people in the theater the illusion of "the inevitable development"; they provide diversion and comfort. No one will take them to task for having complicated the plot they have concocted. When necessary, they will again bring down the deus ex machina, to once more remit their errors and their self-righteous preaching. Only a few will dare say, in an undertone, that the deus ex machina is nothing but a fraud, and that only the worst of dramaturges would use it. Only a few will remonstrate that tomorrow is already here, that the tragic Israeli-Palestinian plot is cyclical, not linear, because its causes are fixed and existential. Everyone will shout them down.

As early as April 1990, a few months before Iraq overran Kuwait, Saddam Hussein threatened Israel with "binary chemical weapons" and bragged of his ability "to burn half of Israel." At the time attention was focused on the Intifada, especially on its murderous manifestations. Not long before, a young Jewish man had fired indiscriminately into a group of Arab laborers, and two Jewish boys had been kidnapped and murdered in Jerusalem. The Iraqi dictator's threats were dismissed as more of the baseless bravado he was known for. The right-wingers who did take note of them were dismissed as warmongers and the enemies of peace. The Palestinians were still playing their cat-and-mouse games with the Israeli army, but were exhausted after thirty months of Intifada; they heeded the voices from the north. The protagonists in the Israeli-Palestinian conflict were ready for the descent of whatever god was on duty, but the chorus was still declaiming the old refrains.

Shortly after Saddam Hussein invaded Kuwait, Knesset members from the parties of the left and from Labor met in Jerusalem with Palestinian leaders from the territories and adopted a "joint statement of principles." The first section of the document stated unambiguously: "The Israeli-Palestinian conflict is the heart of the Middle East problem and must be solved immediately." Some of the less dovish participants wondered whether the document was an analysis of the situation or simply wishful thinking. They wanted a reference to the occupation of Kuwait and "demanded unambiguous condemnation of the action." A Palestinian spokesman told them: "We haven't come here to solve the problems of the world, only the Israeli-Palestinian conflict. . . . The occupation of Kuwait is an internal Arab matter." In the end, the meeting, described as "positive and constructive," did not address the approaching Desert Storm. Those assembled continued to work on "the heart of the matter" and appointed a drafting committee that was supposed to address unresolved questions, such as the Palestinian right of return, the status of the PLO, Jewish immigration, the question of borders, and Israeli security. "We're talking about an exceptional meeting," enthused one of the leading Jewish participants. "If the people who participated were those responsible for reaching a peace agreement, it would happen soon."

But there was no chance at all that those who attended the meeting would ever reach a peace agreement on their own.

When it came down to it, neither the Israeli peace movement nor Palestinian intellectuals directed the drama. The Palestinian public did. The Intifada had taken both the Jewish and the Palestinian participants in the dialogue by surprise. What threatened the status quo was not the publication of statements of principles; it was something spontaneous and "irrational." Most of the Palestinian intellectuals were shunted to the margins, and center stage was taken by the Shock Committees and the Unified Command.

The Palestinian intellectuals spent several months in trauma, after which they managed to find themselves positions as commentators on and propagandists for the Intifada in the West. They were snidely referred to by fellow Palestinians as the "Intifada Notables." The Jewish peace movement and its leaders were stirred by the Intifada, applauding the "anticolonial uprising." Yet they did not and could not do much other than publish fervent articles about it. Their delicate status on the edge of the Jewish consensus did not allow them even to support the Intifada; they could only explain the "inevitable historical process that gave birth to the uprising," a process proving that the Palestinian state would certainly be created. "Everyone knows it will happen," they said. They were condemned to be a background chorus while others determined the drama's development. The Palestinians had never, after all, trusted the peace movement. They conducted dialogues with it, participated in joint delegations, took advantage of its sensitivity to human life and to the denial of human freedom, all in order to raise Palestinian ratings in world public opinion. There were Palestinians who believed there might be a way of reaching the hearts of Likud supporters, but most of them thought that the Jews would not get out of the territories of their own volition and were sure that the status quo could be shattered only by a blow from outside—the charge of an Arab cavalry led by a modern Saladin, or American pressure on Israel.

For years the Palestinians had hoped that their oppression, misery, and sacrifices would spur the entire world to take action. They believed that they need do nothing but appeal to its sense of mercy and its conscience. When they despaired at the Arab and Western world's apathy, they began their uprising. For many months they hoped that the great impact made by their "boys with the stones" would produce political fruit, and that the Arab world would act. In November 1988 they made a great ideological sacrifice and agreed to the partition of Palestine and to the rest of the terminology demanded by the Americans in exchange for "dialogue" with them. Yet nearly two years passed and the "dialogue" produced nothing; then it was terminated. An atmosphere of depression pervaded the territories; young men imposed a reign of terror, and the number of Palestinians killed in assaults by the "shock forces" overtook the number killed by Jewish bullets. This murky atmosphere was broken by a flash of lightning in the form of a new Saladin, a fearless knight who, with the stroke of his sword, would overturn the status quo in the Arabian peninsula and wreak terror on the West. He would then come at the head of his horsemen and destroy the Crusader-Jewish state. "Whoever he may be," a Christian Palestinian journalist wrote in an Israeli newspaper, "he revealed to me something revolutionary and wonderful that is summed up in the traditional motto he adopted—*Allah hua akbar*, Allah is great. That, as I understand it, means faith in the great God, in a God greater than sophisticated aircraft, greater than modern technology, greater than the combined power of the twenty-eight countries that attacked Iraq"—and certainly greater than Israel, that flaccid appendage of the contemptible West.

There is no way of knowing whether Yassir Arafat was carried away by messianic fervor or whether he was being opportunistic when he reached the conclusion that Saddam Hussein would succeed in killing his prey. In any case, he went to Baghdad and kissed his brother, throwing the Palestinian national movement into an incongruity that it would take long to escape. The Palestinians found themselves supporting Iraq's occupation of Kuwait while simultaneously demanding the end of Israel's occupation of the territories. In retrospect, we know that Arafat bet on the wrong horse, but the real damage he caused was to set back the Intifada's achievements. He had not started the uprising, but for many long years he had succeeded in focusing attention inward, on what was happening in the Palestinian homeland, and forcing the world and the Jews to confront the root of the problem. Arafat's embrace of Saddam Hussein returned the PLO and the Palestinians to square one.

Gods from machines may be disguised as new gods, but their role seldom changes. Fifty-five years before, in what the Jews called the "Troubles," the Arabs of Palestine had made a heroic attempt to take their fate into their own hands, to break free of the great and amorphic Arab framework and fight the existential threat presented by Zionism. The unplanned "Arab Rebellion" was, however, doomed from the start. The fragmented Palestinians had no chance against the British army. One thousand days after it began in April 1936, when the plot had thickened into immobility, the deus ex machina appeared in the form of the Arab states, which "suddenly" intervened, allowing the Palestinians to descend from the limb they had climbed out on with their strength and honor barely preserved. Their independent struggle was subsumed by Arab nationalism and eventually reached the point of ignominiously supporting Nazi Germany. Both "independent Palestinian action" and "the collective Arab struggle" failed time and time again, with discouraging regularity, during the second half of the twentieth century—the 1947–49 war, the Nasser period and 1967, the "popular uprising" in the territories and "Black September" (in 1970), the adventurism of the "alternative homeland" in Lebanon, the Intifada, and the collective Arab stand in the peace process.

Each of these swings of the pendulum between the internal Palestinian pole and the pan-Arab pole began and ended with an event that seemed to create a new reality, to be commemorated in one more of those symbolic anniversaries that pack the Arab calendar. The "boys with the stones" and Saddam Hussein were the gods currently on duty in the Palestinian tragedy. Like their predecessors, they symbolized despair, helpless anger, inability to cope with an existential threat. They were evidence that the Palestinians were completely unwilling to recognize the constraints of objective reality, adamant in their belief that they could not compromise in a just cause, and certain that justice would eventually win by the sword.

The Saddam-initiated swing of the pendulum to its pan-Arab role made most Israelis sigh with relief. Now they could perceive the conflict in its pan-Arab guise and view the Palestinians (by their own testimony) as one component of the conflict and not its focus. They could revert to global considerations of an external military threat, of conventional and unconventional war. The strange "war" the stone-throwing Palestinian boys had forced on

Israel, the war that turned a great army into a police force, the war that so contradicted the accepted "doctrine," simply melted away.

"Saddam Hussein did good public relations for some of Israel's defense theses," one military commentator noted. The civil defense authorities issued gas masks. Israel began preparing for war, its fifth or sixth with the Arabs. And when Israel prepares for war, everyone unites; if the Palestinians support the enemy, they can go to hell. The Israeli left was a bit unmannerly, indecorously overeager, in the speed with which it divorced the Palestinians. Not a week had passed since the "historic meeting" with the Palestinian leadership in a neutral hotel in Jerusalem, and now the Israeli left was turning its back on its anticolonial confederates. There are, of course, plenty of historical parallels from the more distant and more recent past that testify to how weak the ideological bond is when national instincts awaken. Yet the left spoke with more than a bit of condescension and a sense of relief. "When you again ask for my sympathy for your 'legitimate rights,' you will discover that your cheers for Saddam Hussein have made me deaf," one said, and added: "If I had supported the establishment of a Palestinian state only because the Palestinians also deserve a state, I would now revoke that support. But I continue . . . because it is my own right to be rid of the occupation and its harmful effects. You may very well deserve the occupation, but we do not. I insist, despite everything, on preserving my humanity, but I do not need Arafat, Hussein, and [Mohammed] Daroushe [leader of the Arab Democratic party] in that supreme effort, which is all mine, and which is nearly inhuman in its humanity."

If anything, the peace movement, which had expressed such

sympathy for the despair that gave birth to the Intifada, should also have expressed sympathy for, or understanding of, the despair that induced the Palestinians to line up behind Saddam Hussein. When it comes down to it, what did the Palestinians do except cheer and make contradictory declarations? The Palestinians' emotional reaction was met with a no less emotional response, and with the same motives. For the Israeli left, the outbreak of the Intifada was a deus ex machina that came to redeem them from the pangs of conscience. For one thousand heroic days, the Intifada had allowed them to live the sweet illusion that the end of the occupation was at hand, and that they need not lift a finger. Had Saddam Hussein not appeared, the members of the Israeli left would have had to invent him. His sudden appearance gave them, and the Palestinians, a way to get off the high limb they were stuck on with what remained of their honor intact. It dulled the pain of their reversal and made it easier for them to retract all their rosy forecasts and learned historical analyses. It allowed them to lose themselves in the embrace of the Israeli consensus.

Yet the eagerness with which the spokesmen for the Zionist left latched on to the Palestinian cheers for the Iraqi leader grew out of a deeper need. With the conflict restored to its interstate dimensions, the left could revert to the view that was mother's milk to the Labor movement. A conflict whose focal point is "external"—between Israel and the "Arab world"—is fought by two collectives, and the question of legitimacy does not threaten the left's universalist-humanistic self-identity. Military-political conflicts of this type do not require soul-searching about moral and ideological questions of the kind raised by the internal, intercommunal conflict. Menachem Begin had forced the internal conflict on Israel. The internalization of the conflict was, for him, a kind of victory for Zionism, and permanent rule by force an inevitable consequence of the consummation of Zionism's goal. On the Zionist left, however, the internalization of the conflict created unresolvable ideological contradictions, which were expressed in bitter disputes over military service in the territories, the Palestinian right of return versus the Jewish Law of Return, the limits of obedience, human rights, and political rights. Saddam Hussein made it possible to revert once again to the sterile vocabulary of interstate disputes and escape the inter-communal conceptual conundrum.

Moreover, since Saddam had externalized the dispute, perhaps the pre-1977 world could be recreated. Yossi Sarid, the classic Labor movement's keeper of the flame, wrote on the eve of the Gulf War: "After the crisis the tables will turn and it will be easier and more practical, in my estimation, to break through the front of the Arab countries. I do not mean to stop the world and get off to wait, because we simply do not have the time. The solution to the Palestinian problem will be a by-product of arrangements with Egypt and Syria, and the Palestinians will not be able to blame anyone but themselves and their leadership."

The government and the right-wing groups represented in it were, of course, most pleased. "Reformed leftists have reached heights that pure rightists may never attain," a right-wing activist noted sarcastically. The government was unafraid of the left, but none of its ministers enjoyed the flagellation of the leftist columnists. They could take good advantage of the left's abdication to tighten the screws on the coercive regime in the territories, knowing that no one would raise a cry. As for Saddam Hussein, one prescient Israeli commented: "The right, well aware of the weight of brutal facts in relations between nations, relies on the ability of a persistent historical fact to gain legitimacy, or at least tacit assent. In this it perceives reality more accurately than those of us who still hope in the depths of their hearts that the outside world will rescue us from the quandaries that are first and foremost our own moral dilemmas."

The right understood the challenge presented by the thief of Baghdad—he was a threat to the status quo in the entire region, not to Israel alone. He endangered the vital interests of the West and of the Arabian peninsula. He evoked the long-standing frustration and anger of millions of Arabs, taunted all authority, and aspired to upset the fragile balance of power that had just barely kept the Middle East from slipping into chaos. It was not only the West that had to respond to this challenge. The regional powers of the status quo also had to react. Ironically, Israel's enemies were willing to consider Israel an integral part of the regional status quo—but only so long as it did not demand a public declaration to that effect, was not contemplating any military response to Iraq's provocations, and continued to occupy itself only with the Palestinians it so badly wanted to control.

The Gulf War was not a renewal of the Israeli-Arab interstate conflict—historical processes never retrace their steps. Saddam Hussein repeated Gamal Abd al-Nasser's slogans: Arab unity and an end to the artificial borders and fictitious sovereign entities created by European imperialism—the root of all the Arab nation's ills. But Saddam Hussein's revisionism appeared an entire generation after the Europeans had gone; his bluster sounded hollow. He was not Nasser, who fought imperialism and defeated it, and neither did he come from Cairo, the Arab world's capital. He did not come to impose order on the inheritance of a recently withered colonialism; rather, he was seeking to challenge a geopolitical system that had already been institutionalized.

Saddam Hussein's very attempt to do so is, paradoxically, evidence of how much the countries of the region, notwithstanding their "artificial" borders, have become defined, viable entities. The Iraqis tried to destroy Kuwait, a sovereign entity lacking any ethnic or historical distinctiveness, a creation of Britain's anachronistic interests. Yet Iraq itself is nothing but a collection of Ottoman provinces that the same European power cobbled together into a political entity for long-obsolete reasons. The artificiality of Iraq's borders and the fact that the majority of its population is composed of ethnic and religious groups that detest the Iraqi Sunni "nation" did not keep Saddam Hussein from putting together a military and political regime that was considered legitimate as long as it did not try to make changes in the name of anti-imperialist ideology. Those who threaten "artificial borders" and "fictitious entities" actually threaten all countries in the region, since which of them (Egypt excepted) is not based on the same fiction that Kuwait is? Whoever chooses to eliminate an Arab state, rather than the "artificial Zionist entity" cannot seriously mean to lead his cavalry to the Holy Land and liberate it from the infidel.

Saddam Hussein did not heed the angry warnings of Arab rulers that his conquest of Kuwait legitimized Israel's conquest of the territories, forced them into an alliance with the West, and thus perpetuated the geopolitical status quo in Palestine. His actions were dictated by the uncontrollable desire of a greedy, power-hungry tyrant. His pan-Arabist and anti-Zionist rhetoric was no more sincere than the Islamic and social-equality blabber he produced. As a result, few Arabs fell for his incitement, and the leaders of Syria, Egypt, and Saudi Arabia in particular took no risks when they allied themselves with the United States against the "sister nation" of Iraq. The consolidation of an international and local coalition was resounding proof of the legitimacy of the existing system and the illegitimacy of the challenge to it.

American rhetoric created the impression that the United States planned to create a "new order" in the Middle East, a Pax Americana. The Americans, so some hoped and so others feared, had come to stay, to impose an era of peace on this conflict-ridden region. But rhetoric is one thing and action another. The Americans acted only after a broad international consensus was reached; they made no move until the United Nations Security Council legitimized their actions. Because they had to bridge over the chasms between various interests, the Americans could act only when the justification for forceful intervention was unambiguous, when legitimate local elements supported it solidly, and when there was a broad national consensus in the United States. The Americans clearly distinguished between violent conflicts among countries—which harm the international system and have political and economic implications for global interests—and chronic internal and intercommunal conflicts. They have learned the lessons of their interventions in Iran and in Lebanon. Only when endemic internal conflicts break out in their backyard—as in Grenada, Panama, and El Salvador—do they allow themselves to intervene. It was not to revise the geopolitical system that they came to the Middle East, but rather to reestablish the status quo and restore the balance of power between the northern and southern parts of the Fertile Crescent and coexistence between desert and settled land. They acted to reaffirm a system that allows collections of tribes disguising themselves as sovereign states to continue to stew in their own juices, just as long as their quarrels pose no danger to world order.

It was not a new world order that was born from the Gulf War—it was the same bad old Middle East reincarnate. It was the same unstable, inflammable system of countries divided within by class, social, and cultural dissension unchanneled into democratic frameworks, tormented by jealousy of their neighbors and fear of the outside world's influence. It was a Middle East dreaming of an apocalypse that would recreate the long-lost Arab Golden Age. Political writers who found the status quo repulsive prepared the audience for a new act in the drama, one in which the long-awaited catharsis would finally take place. The Middle East would no longer be what it was, they said. The approaching war, they wrote, would change the situation fundamentally, bringing in its wake a regional peace imposed by the Americans. The major element in the postwar order would, they hoped, be Israeli withdrawal from the territories.

The Gulf War was seen by many as an opportunity to shatter the enduring status quo in the territories and find a way out of the quicksand of intercommunal conflict. Iraq's threat, and the Palestinians' support for Saddam Hussein, left no doubt in the minds of the left—Israel was once more on the eve of the total war they had "constantly warned" against. The costs of this war, they believed, would force Israeli society into a decision on the issue of the territories—their evacuation. Those who seek war find it, even if it is not their war.

The Likud government, like the left, chose to define the conflict in the Persian Gulf as a war in which Israel was directly involved—but for the opposite reasons. Iraq was a mortal danger, and that galvanized the right. The theses that Israel lived in a hostile world, that it could trust only in itself, and that "the Arabs" want nothing less than the destruction of the Jewish state were proven once again. When faced with such an enemy, there was no room for compromise—certainly not for a territorial compromise that endangered Israel's security. But even as they fostered a sense of public danger, the members of the Likud government hoped that the Gulf conflict might actually strengthen the status quo. The optimal means was to emphasize the danger while also stressing the caution and responsibility called for in making any preemptive military move. The greater the existential danger, the greater the value of restraint would be. Underscoring the fact that Iraq threatened Israel with missiles and weapons of mass destruction would change the image Israel had acquired during the Intifada. Powerful Israel, trampling on the Palestinians, would once more become identified with the persecuted Jews. If it were to sit quiet despite the danger, it would win points with the Americans, and when the dust settled, it would be among those that gained from the reestablishment of the status quo.

Defining the situation as a "state of war" was, then, a result of ideological needs and political considerations more than it was the result of rational military analysis. The minute a potential state of war was announced, expectations began fulfilling themselves. It soon metamorphosed into a "non-conventional" war, gas masks were distributed, and the entire Israeli economy made preparations for a state of emergency. There is ample evidence that the army, the professional body authorized to determine when there is a state of war, and to deal with it subsequently, was suborned by the politicians. Since everyone was afraid of being accused of failure, Israel chose to act on a "worst-case scenario." When Saddam Hussein sent his first barrage of missiles, the worst-case scenario was, so it seemed, confirmed, and Israeli society sank into a paralyzing anxiety.

The authorities took drastic steps and completely disrupted normal routine. Yet closing the schools, halting public transportation, and closing factories had implications beyond the disruption itself. Israeli society, tried in war, instinctively identified the familiar signs of a state of war. In previous wars, however, the disruption was caused by the call-up of the reserves and civilian vehicles, while this time everyone stayed home. This odd "state of war," without a front and without military activity, only a threatened rear and sealed rooms, was a new kind of experience, and so even more threatening. It goes without saying that the warning of a gas attack on Israel led to a panic about mass destruction and conjured up the specter of the Holocaust. This distress and anxiety were doubled and redoubled because the missiles hit Tel Aviv and its suburbs, Israel's soft underbelly. The illusion that ebullient Tel Aviv, that open and hedonistic metropolis, was thousands of miles away from any violent conflict was thunderously shattered. The panicky flight to violent Jerusalem, where the conflict was apparent in every corner, forced many to face up to their existential situation.

This traumatic experience was perceived as an extreme emergency and was officially defined as "war." The Israeli public reacted as it was accustomed to react to war. The sense of a common fate sharpened, the willingness to sacrifice for the general good grew, patriotism and tribal mobilization strengthened. Yet this strange war also awakened contrary feelings. With the entire family cooped up in a sealed room, with no front line and no collective concern for our brave soldiers there, individual anxiety increased, and with it the feeling of each man for himself. The anxiety, the shock, and the reactions to "this war, so different from all its previous ones" did not make people wonder if this was really a war, if the definition fit the objective facts. Saddam Hussein made no hostile move that was a real threat to the Israeli collective—yet only such a threat can be called war. The volleys of missiles that hit civilians and their property were more like acts of terrorism—sporadic violence that serves a political purpose. It was a desperate attempt to create a provocation that would unravel the anti-Iraq coalition.

Saddam Hussein had made a political, not military, move, and by any test Israel was not in a state of war. It is doubtful whether the Iraqis were capable of launching, or would have dared to launch, missiles with the potential for mass destruction. Just as the Intifada was not a war, so neither was firing missiles at Tel Aviv worthy of the name. Worrying about precise, objective definitions might have sounded like a semantic exercise had the definition of the situation not had practical implications and important political consequences. The subjective impression that Israel was in a state of war led to a discussion of the options for a military response, since military aggression must be countered by force. Although it engaged only the civilian sector and lacked a front line, the war "must" turn into a real war, it was thought. The lack of military response made its people feel that Israel had lost its "reputation as a country that never forgives the spilling of its citizens' blood."

Some were astonished by "the new American determination

to establish a new order, including a new form of Israel's use of its own power." A romantic intellectual was jolted out of his illusions: "We are awakening from a long dream to a reality that diminishes our stature in our own eyes. Israel's self-image as a fortress ready for battle is growing blurred and distant." The dilemma—"to give or not to give a fitting response via a large-scale retaliatory action"—was presented as a dilemma with earth-shattering implications; the responsibility placed on the shoulders of Prime Minister Yitzhak Shamir was "of almost equal weight with the one that weighed on David Ben-Gurion's shoulders on the eve of the decision to declare independence," wrote one journalist. The Israeli author A. B. Yehoshua discerned "the now clarifying totality of our conflict. . . . the range of the Israeli-Arab conflict has become total, beginning as it does from the smallest and most intimate knifing incident, through bombs, rockets, tanks, and airplanes, through the next missile that comes from above the atmosphere (today from Iraq, tomorrow perhaps from Iran or Libya). And, after all, we love to be distinctive. Here, they've already found us a small distinction in our struggle that, in my humble opinion, does not exist in any other known conflict in history" (*Politika*, no. 37 [March 1991]).

The knife and the missile combined into an apocalyptic threat that was "a mortal danger to Israel," more serious than just any war. Commentators, politicians, and columnists used war images to analyze "the situation." But, strangely enough, ordinary people understood that this strange war was not their war. Eighty percent of the Jewish residents of Israel preferred "restraint," and this number did not change during the course of the war. "Righteous people's work is done by others," many said, and believers saw God acting in history.

The government, ostensibly facing a world-shaking dilemma, acted the only way open to it—it abstained from any military intervention. Any response to Saddam Hussein's provocation would have played into his hands, and the results would potentially have been catastrophic. The international coalition did not need Israel, and the Americans made every possible military effort to eliminate the missile threat and so preclude any possible motive for—or pressure on Israel to stage—a response that would be embarrassing for the United States and its coalition partners. This "state of war" simply did not fit the script of the interstate war, repeating itself each decade since 1948. "The totality of the knife and the missile"—or to put it simply, the cause-and-effect relationship between the local intercommunal conflict and the total, interstate conflict—existed only in the fertile minds of observers who wanted the Gulf War to reestablish the international dimension of the Israeli-Arab conflict.

This struggle had begun a hundred years before in ethnic strife and expanded in ever-widening circles, from a conflict between neighbors, shepherds, farmers, and watchmen, to local intercommunal riots, and from there to a civil war that engulfed the entire country, and during which neighboring countries joined the circle of violence, making it into a war between regular armies. In the 1980s, after Israel reached a peace agreement with the largest of its enemies, the conflict slowly returned to its original dimensions, but despite the fact that its range was reduced, its force and depth were not. The Intifada and the knifings, the slingshot and the club, the rubber bullet and the prison camp were its manifestations.

Now people wanted to declare a change "from the knife to the missile." The conflict once more acquired regional, interstate dimensions. The "proof" was the way Palestinians behaved during the war. Not only did they support and cheer Saddam Hussein; they even went up to their roofs and applauded at the sight of the missiles landing on Tel Aviv. They and Saddam were one. The transition from the knife, from the violence of one body touching another, to the inhuman missile that comes down "from beyond the atmosphere," brought with it—paradoxically—a sense of relief. After all, when a missile was fired, someone turned on a siren and ordered people to enter their sealed rooms; there was no warning when a demented knifer attacked. The fear of the missile was collective, and there was comfort in mass anxiety. People did not see the murder in the enemy's eyes. He remained there, over the horizon, not at the front gate. The primal shepherds' fistfight that had raged for three years had turned into a "total conflict"; now we were part of "the region."

"In one fell swoop Saddam Hussein's defective, inferior missiles made us part of the region . . . so that our sky is no longer ours alone," a columnist wrote. "Now we are not the only ones who can strike a blow in the Middle East. The Middle East can strike at us also." How convenient it was to exchange the visible enemy, the conflict over a swatch of land and a street corner, for a conflict over the "sky [that] is no longer ours alone" and an impersonal, geographically defined enemy. One perceptive Israeli said: "We are once more tasting collective fear . . . that is a very elementary taste, drawn from primal depths. But to the people of Zion it is sweet, sweeter than the tense routine, than the unending oppression, than the exhausting mechanism of psychological repression."

The "total" experience gave rise to a longing for a total solution. "We must be certain that we leave no clear and unjustified provocation that will feed Satanic thoughts against us," said A. B. Yehoshua. "We must broaden the circle of countries that will do everything they can to prevent war in the region, war that will be catastrophic for them as well. . . . It is within our ability . . . to bring the Palestinians [in] as partners in peace and development."

The speed with which the anxiety and shock dispersed testifies to just how this strange war was in the end not "the cause and catalyst of social processes." Rather, it remained in the memory of the Israeli public only as a bad dream, a somewhat embarrassing attack of neurosis, of which one should be ashamed. What could be more symbolic of the reality than the fact that the morning after the Gulf War cease-fire, a young Jewish man was stabbed to death in the streets of Jerusalem's Old City, and that on the day of U.S. Secretary of State James Baker's arrival in Jerusalem, a young Arab murdered four women at a bus stop? There it was—from the knife to the missile—and back.

The trauma of the Gulf War had real long-range emotional, ideological, and political ramifications only in the context of the Israeli-Palestinian intercommunal conflict. This in and of itself is evidence that the thesis of "totality" is unsound and confirms the thesis that the "internal" conflict model has not changed. It is only natural that fear and hatred of the enemy pushed hawkish right-wing dispositions to the extreme. Such people's sense of hostility to "the Arabs" in general focused on the Palestinians, both because they supported the Iraqis and expressed their joy at Israel's misfortunes under bombardment and because they were there. The level of this hostility may be measured by public opinion surveys, but it may well be that the reactions of liberals, who are sensitive to xenophobia, are the most accurate measurement. One columnist wrote: "It has been years since I have so questioned my political beliefs. . . . I discovered, to my horror, that on many things I am no longer able to give my opinion immediately. . . . I oppose the curfew in the territories, I believe it is inhuman, but I can't say that I long to see 120,000 laborers from the territories walking freely through the streets of our tense city. . . . I always knew that there is a Kahane in the heart of each of us. Racism, hatred of the foreigner, the fear of him, are natural to us—rightists and leftists both, whether we are foolish or intelligent. . . . I admit that this war has put that dark racist in my heart to a severe test. Just a little bit more and he would have emerged."

The government could not do a thing against the external enemy, but it could act against the internal enemy. When Operation Desert Storm began, a general curfew was imposed on the territories, which lasted for forty-five days. The West Bank and Gaza Strip were put under siege, and two million people were shut up in their homes. Economic activity came to a total halt, thousands of people were detained, and many went hungry. The human suffering was unbearable; even security considerations in wartime did not justify the steps taken. No one had any doubt that the government was imposing a collective punishment in reaction to the Palestinians' support for Saddam Hussein.

The draconian measures taken elicited almost no protest from the liberal side of the Jewish community. The liberals considered these necessary wartime measures, and a fitting response to the Palestinians' elation at the bombardment of Jewish areas. "They danced on the rooftops" was the often-repeated justification for an additional fudging of universal values. The Jewish consensus was prepared to grant legitimacy to harsh repression, and there was no outcry at the trampling of human rights. The government's measures stifled the violence. In fact, during the war, almost no violent incidents were recorded in the territories. It was possible to live in the illusion that "there is no way back to the period of the stone and the Intifada." Intellectuals praised Israel's "self-restraint" (using a Hebrew term employed for the Yishuv's policy of self-restraint in the face of Arab attacks during the 1936 Arab uprising). "It may well be that it is part of our process of maturation . . . It seems to me that had it not been for the war in Lebanon, we would not have seen the reserve we see in this war. The aggregate experience of this government pointed it toward restraint," said one Israeli intellectual. Another hoped that "the children who lived through this restrained war will see, perhaps, that it is possible to prepare—not to react immediately, to shoot from the hip . . . if they absorb this, that self-restraint is not weakness, then the war will have one welcome result."

Of course, the "welcome outcome" referred to the lack of a military response to the missile bombardment. This "commendable restraint" did not apply to the drastic repressive measures in the territories, where it was permissible to react "immediately, to shoot from the hip," without considering the results or the "complexity of the situation." Only a few warned that "the real test of society is preserving its fundamental values of justice precisely at a time of crisis and distress." It is easy to ascribe moral and historical meanings to "self-restraint" when it is dictated by objective constraints. But the moral test of the use of force, as with every moral test, comes when a country is free to choose whether or not to use it.

A new wave of brutal murders punctured the illusion of "the end of the Intifada." Return to the routine intercommunal conflict was unbearable; the public was fed up with knifings, with terrorist infiltration, and with Molotov cocktails; it was ready for drastic measures. Accordingly, it was tempting to endorse plans boasting that they could cure the internal conflict by drastic surgery (these plans and their implementation will be discussed below). The major hope for deliverance focused, however, on the peace process. Those who believed that the Middle East would no longer be what it had been, and that the regional and internal status quo had been shattered by the thunder of the missiles, waited breathlessly for the Americans to act. The reinstatement of the interstate dimension of the conflict and the alliance of the United States with the moderate Arab states created, so they wanted to believe, a golden opportunity for a comprehensive peace process to succeed, and a solution to "the Palestinian problem" would be a "by-product" of that process.

The Americans did, in fact, launch a new and much-trumpeted peace process. Secretary of State James Baker began a shuttle tour, and the chefs at the King David Hotel in Jerusalem learned to prepare his favorite dishes. At first it seemed as if the American peace initiative was merely routine, and that its fate would be no different from those other of American peace initiatives, which seemed to come along two or three times a decade. But it slowly became clear that this initiative was different from its predecessors. In the past, the Americans had begun the diplomatic process after some outbreak of violence between Israel and its neighbors. This time the initiative sprang from the United States's own needs. The link between the present peace process and the Gulf War was the plight of President Bush, who had sown a storm and reaped only wind.

Desert Storm was exactly what its code name implies—a sudden, mighty blast of wind, clouds of dust swirling in a vast expanse, billows of dust and blinding sand—and silence. The wilderness, which had suddenly come to life, returned to its eternal silence as if nothing had happened. Its inhabitants emerged from their hiding-places, shook off the sand, and returned to their daily routines: the struggle over wells and grazing, brutal fistfights between shepherds, tribal alliances made and broken, a longing for the unachievable tranquility of the desert oasis—and endless palavers around the campfire.

The Americans did a good job of camouflaging the movements of their army, and the goals of the war as well. But the day the cease-fire was declared, the truth was exposed in all its cunning. The declarations of "a crusade to depose the Iraqi dictator" and "a new world order" were nothing but rhetoric to raise the morale of the troops and to convince them that the cause was just. American's real goal in the war was the reimposition of the status quo ante—including leaving Saddam Hussein in place. According to explicit instructions from Washington, the commanders of Desert Storm allowed the major part of Saddam's army to escape the American encirclement and return to Baghdad, so ensuring that the Iraqi regime would retain its power base.

The Shiites in southern Iraq and the Kurds in the north paid a heavy and bloody price for having believed the American declarations, and for having deluded themselves into thinking that a new era that would include their independence had really begun in the Middle East. Only when it became clear how great the Kurdish tragedy was, when the United States could no longer take the international criticism of its hypocrisy, did the Americans intervene, take minimal steps to ease the plight of hundreds of thousands of refugees, and create safe havens for Kurds in northern Iraq.

A new norm had been established—that the international community could force a sovereign state to dismantle destructive and strategic weapons under close supervision. A precedent was also set—that an aggressive state may be disciplined for an attempt to eliminate another country. Yet another new norm had also made its appearance—the international community can intervene in the internal affairs of sovereign states if the UN Security Council determines that serious violations of human rights therein constitute a threat to world peace. The precedent established in Iraq would soon be followed up in Somalia, and later in Haiti, where even human suffering and usurpation of power constituted reasons for international intervention.

But in the Middle East everything reverted too quickly to the way it had been before, and people began to wonder if there had really been a war, and where the new world order was. President Bush and his aides could not bear the derision and the disappointment. They had to prove that the war had produced something lasting. What could be more convincing than a declaration that they had succeeded in resolving the most famous of all disputes—the Israeli-Arab conflict? It was of utterly no consequence that this old struggle had absolutely no connection with the frustration of Iraqi aggression, and that during the war, Bush had himself denied any link between it and Desert Storm. (Quite the opposite—it had been Saddam Hussein who had tried to link the two, much to the indignation of other Arab leaders.)

The average American is naturally not an expert on the political intricacies and geography of the Middle East. Because of the Israeli-Arab conflict's constant press exposure and the missile attacks on Tel Aviv, it was thus very easy to create a fictitious but persuasive circumstantial connection between the Gulf War and the Israeli-Arab struggle. Historians and experts might raise their eyebrows and point out how arbitrary the links were, but when the president of the United States—and especially a president of the only remaining superpower who has just won a war—wants to create an arbitrary linkage, it's hard to argue with him. His will turns into a hard political fact, which must be confronted—not only by the experts, but also, and especially, by the heads of the client states that live in America's shadow.

The end of the competition between the superpowers left the United States as the only global power and created a new world order with new political constraints—and everyone had to adjust to them. The new situation was not the outcome of the Gulf War, but rather the opposite—it facilitated the consolidation of an international coalition that provided an umbrella of legitimacy without which President Bush could not have defeated the Iraqis. The Arab countries that joined the coalition were a vital element, inasmuch as they legitimized Desert Storm, winning points with the Americans in the process. But in addition to this, each country had its own specific goal. Egypt wanted to return to the Persian Gulf and to the center of the Arab arena. It also wanted to ensure that America would continue to throw money into the bottomless pit of Egyptian needs. The Syrians saw an opportunity to rid themselves of Iraq, their traditional enemy, and also to exploit the opportunity to make a grab in Lebanon. The moment had finally come when they could officially establish without censure that Lebanon had become a Syrian protectorate. Even Jordan, which had supported Iraq and suffered the consequences during the war, emerged unscathed. No Arab country wanted to see Jordan destroyed or to replace the Hashemites in their traditional role as neighbors and partners of the Jewish state. Neither did the Israelis want a different neighbor on their border. Jordan survived, in other words, because it was there, and the status quo continued by default; no one was eager to change it. All the actors took their shares of the spoils. The Israelis had demonstrated self-restraint, and their work was done for them by others. The Egyptians had half of their huge foreign debt eliminated. Kuwait's Amir al-Sabah and his numerous relatives returned to their palaces and their old ways, as did the Saudis. The Turks got their quid pro quo too.

In fact, everyone won except the Palestinians, who had once again bet on the wrong horse. When Secretary of State Baker began his shuttle diplomacy, everyone immediately began presenting promissory notes from the war for redemption—except for the Palestinians, of course, who had run up a heavy debt. There were some encouraging signs: the mere fact that the Arab countries wanted the Americans to redeem their notes; their willingness to discuss "peace"; the agreement that the Palestinian problem should be discussed in the context of the old Camp David formulations. It quickly became clear, however, that each party was agreeing to "peace" on its own terms—that is, provided only the other side would pay for it. The game of musical chairs proceeded according to the rules—when the music stopped, someone would be left on the floor. Each participant continued to circle as the American music played; each player implored the Americans not to stop the music, lest he be declared the loser. The historic "window of opportunity" started looking more and more like the sealed windows of the recent past; some of the players were basing their tactics on the assumption that this peace process would go the way of its predecessors.

It was Syria's president, Hafiz al-Asad, the most seasoned and crafty of them all, who first realized what had happened. This time the peace process arose from President Bush's urgent needs. Whoever aided Bush would be rewarded, whoever interfered would be punished. Al-Asad understood the great opportunity available to him at this critical moment—just as his Russian patrons had walked out and left him naked. Ever resourceful, he grasped that he now had to become an American client; he therefore agreed to the formula offered him. In exchange for his willingness to negotiate directly with Israel (which was termed a "historic step"), he could expect a suitable reward. The Americans would anoint him as a man of peace, would ignore the arsenal of missiles he had acquired and the dictatorial and brutal character of his regime. They would grant him financial aid, and perhaps even force Israel to give him back the Golan Heights.

For a long time the Israeli government stuck with its old tactics—it played for time. The Israelis knew the Americans and how they went about things. The diffuse, pluralist character of American politics and the endless complexity of the American economy made it impossible for a U.S. president to put together anything more lasting than a short-term consensus, one that could do little more than emit brief pulses of energy. These pulses were very potent, but the political power that created them found it hard to generate the chain reactions needed to make them effective in the long term. The Americans, the Israelis knew, would not stay in a losing game. Sooner or later they would grow tired of it and turn to areas in which they were more likely to succeed.

In the meantime, the Israeli government deployed a mixture of deceit and deception, acting as if it had been robbed, or like an unpaid creditor. At the height of the Gulf War, Israel even tried to collect protection money for its noninvolvement, only to be publicly censured for doing so. At the end of the war, it played the injured party at not having been recognized for its decisive contribution to the allied victory. Knowing that without them there could not be even the pretense of a peace process, the Israelis presumed to dictate who could and could not participate in the negotiations and demanded that their preconditions be accepted, while those of the other side were rejected. Only Israelis would have the right to determine what was to be linked to what. For instance, only if Saudi Arabia participated would Israel agree to hold discussions with a Jordanian-Palestinian delegation (so long as it contained no PLO representative and no resident of East Jerusalem) at a one-time "non-binding" regional meeting, on condition that the Americans promise in advance that no decisions contrary to Israel's position be taken, that Europe have only observer status, that the Soviet Union participate in the talks only after it recognized Israel, and that the United Nations not have any official status.

Secretary of State Baker needed nerves of steel to cope with these Byzantine intricacies. But what really rankled Baker was when Israel pursued its old negotiating tactic of establishing facts on the ground. The new American peace initiative was, like its predecessors, a catalyst for the establishment of settlements in the territories. Those who followed American peace initiatives could see a correlation between them and the rate at which physical and political faits accomplis have appeared in the occupied territories. When the Rogers Plan was visited upon Israel in 1969, the government reacted by planning and beginning construction of 25,000 apartments in Jerusalem, beyond the Green Line. The separation-of-forces agreements in 1974 accelerated the settlement process that demolished the Allon Plan. The signing of the peace agreement with Egypt and the beginning of the autonomy negotiations in 1979 brought about the expropriation of half of the West Bank's land, the establishment of many scores of settlements, the annexation of the Golan Heights, and the enactment of the "Jerusalem Law." The Reagan initiative of 1982 brought about a doubling of Jewish settlements in the territories.

This tactic (or perhaps this instinctive reaction) was at work again in 1991, but this time at an unprecedented level. The Israelis began an operation to double the Jewish population of the occupied territories within four years. They anticipated a lukewarm reaction from the Americans of the "settlements are an obstacle to peace" type; when the Americans complained that the continuation of settlement activity was a provocation sabotaging the peace process, the Israelis rolled their eyes and wondered why the settlement of their homeland was being linked to the peace process. They still did not discern the fundamental difference between this peace process and its predecessors. This time the provocation was directed, not at the Arabs, but at the president of the United States himself. This misunderstanding would cost them dearly, but the actual price tag would become clear only at the beginning of autumn. In the meantime the Syrian president's consent forced the Israelis to overcome their hesitations and declare their willingness to participate in a "regional conference" and negotiate unconditionally with the Syrians. Of course, they continued to trust the Palestinians to save them by presenting inflexible positions.

At the end of 1991, the curtain fell on the Gulf War act, but not on its epilogue. Saddam Hussein, the deus ex machina, son of Satan, appeared, did what he did, and dissolved into thin air (for the present). Behind the scenes, the next act was already being concocted, one that would console the multitudes and bring them hopes of a bright future. Those most in need of consolation were the Palestinians.

The spring and summer of 1991 were among the harshest and most bitter in the chronicle of the Palestinian people's tragedy. At a single blow, two of their greatest hopes of redeeming their fortunes were shattered. The first, Saddam Hussein, exploded in thunder; the second, the Intifada, seemed to have petered out with a whimper. The pathetic end of the "mother of all wars" was a shock for the Palestinians; the humiliation hurt them more than anything else. "For me, as a patriotic Arab, the hardest thing to take was the picture of the Iraqi prisoners kissing the hands of their captors while an American officer threw them bread as if they were his dogs," said one Palestinian. He added: "The Iraqis' empty shoes in the sand reinforced the stereotype of the cowardly Arab. Every realistic person was aware that the forces were skewed, but we hoped that at least there would be a battle that would prove that the Arab fighter is worth something, that would show that the Arab has something to say." In a society guided by concepts of honor and shame, the disgrace was unbearable.

The humiliation, confusion, and puzzlement were as great as the expectations had been. "What about Arafat's declaration that Abu Oudai [Saddam Hussein] would soon be praying at al-Aqsa? . . . Leaders must not deceive nations," said an Israeli Arab member of the Knesset. Many were unwilling to accept defeat. A mechanism of denial and repression was in action, just as it had been after every Arab defeat. Many believed that Saddam had not been defeated, but had rather held his own against the entire world—after all, he was still in power. There were those who considered the cease-fire only one stage in an engagement that would end in an Arab victory. Only a handful tried to learn from the experience. "The defeat is, when it comes down to it, the defeat of the Arab man, who has always been his own most dangerous enemy. Were we to teach the Arab individual to fight against blind obedience, not to pass silently over iniquity and to protest injustice, maybe things would be different." But the majority searched for "objective" excuses: "It was not a war of Islam against Christianity, but more of a war of the industrialized, northern world against the southern, poor world." In other words, once again the West was the aggressor and the East the victim.

The defeat brought on a great ideological disorientation. The political-ideological factions united in the Palestine Liberation Organization emerged from the Gulf War beaten and battered. Their leader, Yassir Arafat, who had promised them that the way to Jerusalem passed through Kuwait, was after the war ostracized and vanquished, perhaps even more so than his patron, Saddam. The nationalists' bitter opponents, the Islamic fundamentalists, also found their prophets proven false. Their clergy had promised them the victory of the true faith and great miracles, but instead it was the American infidel who had won. The ideological distress in both camps created severe internal tensions, but the sense of humiliation strengthened the fundamentalists, who were a refuge for the frustrated.

The political struggle between the nationalist Palestinian factions and the Islamicists had begun even before the Intifada. As early as the late 1970s, and especially at the beginning of the 1980s, there was a strong movement back to religion, expressed in a dramatic rise in the number of worshipers in mosques and in the public observance of religious precepts (the prohibition against eating and smoking in public during the holy month of Ramadan, modest dress for women, beards for men). Islamic leagues, which had existed throughout the occupied territories, but had been especially active in the Gaza Strip, grew and expanded. Together with working to develop religious and social services, these associations began voicing a political message that was a sharp challenge to the Palestinians' national movement, the PLO. The attack was not only ideological; battle was joined for the hearts of the Palestinian masses.

The Israeli authorities saw the fight brewing, and being concerned with suppressing PLO activity and pursuing al-Fatah's terrorist cells, they believed that support for political Islam would serve their purposes. Yet this "divide and rule" strategy was not fruitful; in fact, it boomeranged. The Islamic movement's religious and social activity built up a strong political movement, which had terrorist cells of its own from its very inception. The militant Islamic movement Hamas offered the Palestinians a political message according to which nationalism had failed and only religion could succeed. It preached violent resistance to the occupation and rejected any peace that would leave any holy Islamic land in the hands of the Jews. But more than anything else, it painted a new picture of the world, spoke in a new political language, and advocated a different national culture and a different way of life.

In this sense, Hamas resembled the burgeoning Islamic fundamentalist movements in the rest of the region. Islamic fundamentalism moved into the vacuum left by the bankruptcy of etatist-socialist pan-Arabism. Its militant character derived from its being an expression of the deep frustration of the underprivileged. It therefore necessarily rejected the entire established order. Large groups, especially among the unemployed and impoverished urban proletariat and the frustrated lower middle class, were willing to listen to the arguments of religious zealots from outside the official religious establishment. They told the masses that Islam was a solution for their personal troubles, for society's ills, for the economic and moral bankruptcy of the regime, and for their own sense of helplessness when faced with the inability of the Arab world to compete with the West.

Hamas's rise was directly linked to the worsening economic situation and to the accumulated frustration and degradation of the ongoing occupation. The reservoir of human misery concentrated in the Gaza Strip produced most of the Hamas terrorist cells responsible for the murder of Israelis, as well as the self-motivated lone knifers who attack Israelis on the streets. "The typical knifer is an indigent laborer, unmarried, living in an extremist Muslim atmosphere, sometimes even exploited by Muslim zealot organizations, and he is a daily participant in the gauntlet of humiliation on the way to the [Israeli] labor market" (Ilan Pappe, *Profil shel sakinay* [Profile of a Stabber] [Givat Haviva, 1993]; in Hebrew).

The Israelis, who quickly recovered from the delusion that they could play Hamas against the PLO, began to identify fundamentalism as their most dangerous enemy. They naturally tried to understand the fundamentalist enemy in his general context. For them, the rise of Hamas is the inevitable outcome of the rising power of fundamentalism throughout the region. Therefore, Israelis reason, their enemy is also the enemy of the Arab regimes and the West. But the background is, of course, entirely different. The Islamic groups fighting Israel are joined in a battle against the occupation and against the Jewish people; Islam is, at least in the short run, a means and not an end. The parallel Israelis draw between Egypt's and Algeria's war against their fundamentalists and Israel's struggle against Hamas is ludicrous. In Arab countries, militant Islam is calling for a change of regime and a new social order for its own people, whereas in Israel it is fighting for the expulsion of a detested foreign conqueror.

Antagonism between the nationalists and the Islamicists was not sharp at the beginning of the Intifada, but it grew stronger as the Intifada went on and hopes dwindled. The debate over Palestinian participation in the peace talks has increased their mutual hostility.

It may well be that the power struggles between Hamas and al-Fatah were unconnected to the Iraqi defeat in the Gulf War, but the bloody confrontations between the two groups in the summer of 1991 were evidence that the national solidarity that characterized the Intifada is weakening. Palestinian violence was directed inward. The number of Palestinians killed by their own people in the summer of 1991 was almost three times the number killed by the Israeli army.

Such infighting was not new; what was new was the public airing the Palestinians gave it. This internal terror was the object of open, pointed criticism from Palestinian leaders, as was the uncontrolled behavior of the "masked killers" who perpetrated it. The Palestinians embarked on a public discussion of whether the Intifada should change its tactics. They searched their souls under the guise of a "reexamination." One of them said: "If there is not a significant change in the pursuit of the struggle and there is not a new strategy for the Intifada, Palestinian society will turn fascist." Another said: "The Intifada should be a constructive force. We must work every day from sunrise to sunset in order to construct the foundations for the state to be."

Most speakers and writers praised the beginning of the Intifada—the general mobilization, the mass demonstrations, the impact on world public opinion—while lamenting its later manifestations—internal terror, the rule of the street by boys, and total anarchy. Hundreds of dead, thousands of wounded, and tens of thousands of prisoners, the devastation of the economy and the drop in the standard of living, the destruction of education, the horrible human suffering—none of these brought lasting political gains. The PLO's support of Saddam Hussein brought the status of the Palestinian nation and its leadership to its lowest ebb. The Israeli occupation remained in place, and it became clear that disengagement from Israel was untenable.

Israel could manage without the Palestinians, but the Palestinians could not survive without Israel. The high-sounding declarations that the Palestinians had erected a physical infrastructure for the state-to-be was nothing but a hollow boast. In the summer of 1991, the number of residents of the occupied territories employed in Israel was almost the same as the number before the Gulf War. Workers continued to go to Israel even on days when there was a general strike—a phenomenon unheard of during the Intifada. At the same time, violent acts against Israelis, sometimes involving the use of firearms, continued.

The despair was reflected in the Palestinians' pessimism about the peace process. This public, which in 1988 had forced the

PLO to adopt realistic positions and showed willingness to make political and symbolic concessions, now took a tough stand. Public opinion polls and public statements showed that a majority of the Palestinians did not believe that a peace conference would succeed, and even opposed Palestinian participation in one under the humiliating conditions dictated by Israel. The Palestine National Council made a series of decisions in September 1991 that authorized Palestinian participation in the diplomatic process, but as during the Intifada, this process was out of touch with the mood in the territories.

There were Israelis who rushed to declare that the Intifada had ended. Others claimed that it had metamorphosed, not died. Everyone agreed, however, that its root causes had not changed and that the violence would continue, even if it were expressed in other ways. "The Intifada has become a way of life," maintained observers who had not long before diagnosed it as a "third front" and "war in a new form." In doing so, they concurred, after the fact, in the conclusion that the Intifada was the outbreak of an intercommunal struggle—a chronic, endemic condition. They also agreed that this struggle would continue, because the Palestinians had crossed the threshold of community mobilization, and having consolidated their community, there was no way back.

In the summer of 1991, it became clear that the self-serving predictions of the collapse of the status quo had not come true. No one had the strength, however, to deal with an endemic conflict such as the Israeli-Palestinian shepherds' war. Israeli officials censured the American secretary of state for "always coming to Israel on the eve of holidays." If he would only tone down his

CHAPTER FIVE

THE ELUSIVE PEACE

Saddam Hussein came and went, and James Baker engaged in months of shuttle diplomacy. His trips were marked by an impressive array of leaks, by an attempt to compartmentalize the issues, and by verbal gymnastics. His method was to condemn the bad guy (whoever they were at the moment), make fuzzy promises, and, especially, stubbornly insist on an artificial target date, which was meant to create the sense that here was a one-time opportunity not to be missed. This flurry of activity demonstrated deep American involvement, but there was no evidence of the kind of imperial resolve necessary to impose a Pax Americana. Had the Bush administration intended to impose a peace, it would not have frittered away its prestige with interminable shuttle trips and Byzantine negotiations with the region's most experienced hagglers. The pose of being an "impartial mediator," and U.S. efforts to drag the rivals to a peace conference even without an agenda, gave cause to suspect that what the Bush administration really wanted was to create the impression that it was making peace while avoiding the unpleasant necessity of actually doing so. Nevertheless, and perhaps precisely because of this, the Americans did not doubt that everyone would show up at the peace conference at the end of October 1991, even if up until the last minute no one could agree on where it would be.

The puerile bargaining over the conference site was merely the tail end of a campaign of reciprocal pressure and intimidation by the participants that left behind it a long trail of obscure "working papers" and oral agreements. These were lumped together under the name of the "Madrid formula." Nor did the horse-trading stop when the conference was called. There were contradictory interpretations of the letters of invitation before they had even been written up. Typically, the parties to the negotiations demanded and received letters of assurance; the Americans handed these out to everyone to mollify them. Since all the fundamental issues were in dispute, the only way the Americans could placate the parties was to write ambiguously. Their method was to quote selectively from international documents like the Camp David agreements. To the Palestinians they quoted the first part of a clause that speaks of transferring power during an interim stage in which the Palestinians would accustom themselves to exercising authority on the West Bank and in Gaza. To the Israelis they quoted the last part of the same clause, so that the Israelis could understand that the transfer of authority meant "full autonomy for the inhabitants"—in other words, that the negotiations for the interim stage would not necessarily lead to a "full transfer of authority."

These fundamental differences were swept under the luxurious carpet of the royal palace in Madrid. No one expected this peace conference to deal with fundamental issues. It was conducted precisely as planned by its producer and director, James Baker. He wanted a ceremonial event, intentionally cut off from reality. He created a sterile world of the type so cherished by the VIP subculture. The delegates were made to feel that they had been invited to join a select club. This went first and foremost to the heads of the newest members, the Palestinians, who had won provisional membership in a Jordanian-Palestinian delegation. How they enjoyed the formalities, the procedural victories, the sympathy of the media, the very fact that they were treated as equals! Ironically, they expressed themselves in terms plagiarized from Zionist history. "In Madrid," one of them said, paraphrasing Theodor Herzl's remark at the end of the First Zionist Congress, "we founded the Palestinian state."

The Americans believed that the sterile world they had created was more realistic than reality itself. Their conflict-resolution experts told them that the most important thing was to seat the opponents around a table; the very fact of contact would create a "positive dynamic." The most pathetic of all were the "Soviets," as they were then called, who escaped for a day or two from Moscow as it prepared for a cold and hungry winter. How pleasant it was for them to bask, even for a moment, in the eminence that had once been theirs, and that had now been momentarily restored to them by grace of the Americans.

The rules imposed by the Americans created, during four long and well-photographed days, a procedural and symbolic symmetry between the Israelis and the Palestinians. The huge discrepancy in physical power and the asymmetry of their international standing were nullified, or so it seemed. The representatives of the subject Palestinian community sat as equals among the representatives of sovereign nations. In fact, in the surrealist conditions that prevailed in Madrid, the Palestinians' weakness was their source of strength and the secret of their propaganda advantage. This symmetry was seen by many as the irreversible essence of this historic event. The Israeli public was beside itself, the left most of all. "History is potent; it has direction, and it has meaning," declared the author A. B. Yehoshua, the major speaker at the Peace Now demonstration on the eve of the Madrid conference. History's direction was obvious—the Gulf War and the end of the Cold War had created conditions that "had" to bring peace between Israel and its neighbors. Better that Israel should not wait for American pressure, which "had" to come. "Better for peace to come out of our internal desire for it rather than by being imposed from outside," Yehoshua said. He believed that an inner desire for peace indeed existed, because "a hundred years is long enough a time to ripen this conflict to the point of solution. It's already so ripe it's rotten."

Faith and hope found expression in messianic terms, pervaded by an apocalyptic atmosphere: "As the world order has changed, so has the face of the Middle East. Here, also, the time has finally come to stop dying and start living," wrote Amos Oz, who concluded his speech with the traditional *shehehayanu* prayer— "Blessed art Thou, O Lord our God, for having preserved us, for having sustained us, and for having brought us to this time." "A historic day, on which the process that will determine eternity began," said Ezer Weizmann, soon to become president of Israel, and Yehoshua openly declared: "Peace Now. That is our messiah."

One does not inquire into the messiah's background: "Peace with the PLO or without the PLO, with Jordan or without Jordan, with all of the Golan Heights or with only half the Golan Heights, via an interim autonomy or in a single, comprehensive step. We are silent now." They yearned for peace as the realization of a prophetic vision, not as a system of concrete arrangements tied down to the real world. Nor did one complain about the messiah's herald, Yitzhak Shamir. True, everyone knew that his positions were frustrating any real chance for peace, but the deus from the machina was even stronger than Shamir: "From these talks something new and true will be born." "Had" to be born, responded the observers and commentators who were covering the peace conference. Every crisis and every hurdle was "on the path of inevitable progress." Who could repudiate so fierce a faith?

It is critical to understand the special importance that Israelis attributed to the peace process and bilateral, face-to-face talks with the Arabs. Arabs negotiating directly with Israel legitimize the Jewish state. By sitting down with authorized Israeli representatives, they recognize the Israeli collective, with its symbols of identification and its national aspirations. The yearning for legitimacy is translated into terms of renunciation by the Arabs of the attempt to destroy Israel and their acknowledgement that the Jewish state is an "established fact." Yet it also subsumes something more fundamental: acceptance of the Zionist enterprise. This is how Amos Oz understood the Madrid conference: "Here, our enemies are finally coming to us, not with missiles and tanks but with documents and provisions. Those who for more than one hundred years demanded that we disappear, evaporate, die, now ask for compromises and concessions. In doing so they openly acknowledge, in the full light of day, that Israel is an established fact. . . . We may well be happy. Not euphoric, but justifiably happy—as those who have achieved in one hundred years more than our fathers ever dreamed of. We may proceed with self-confidence, having believed even in the days when it was very hard to do so that the day would come when the whole world would accept the Zionist enterprise, that the day would come when even the enemy would accept the Zionist enterprise. And here, that day has arrived." It should be noted that the Arabs do not dream of "accepting the Zionist enterprise." Their goal is nothing more than to get back that part of their homeland most recently occupied by the Israelis, in exchange for which they are willing to recognize Israel as an established fact.

This longing for legitimacy beats in the heart of every Israeli. For this reason, most of them termed the Madrid conference—and even more so, the bilateral talks—"historic events." The need for the Arabs' full and final recognition was so strong that the Madrid conference made people forget that for more than a decade there had been peace between Israel and the largest Arab nation, perhaps the only Arab nation worthy of the name "nation." This inner need also explains Israeli officials' pathetic attempts during the conference to make conversation with Arab diplomats, journalists, and officials—anyone, as long as they were Arabs.

The need for legitimacy resounds even more strongly in Israelis on the liberal left. And even greater than their satisfaction over the legitimacy granted the Palestinians was their satisfaction over the legitimacy the Palestinians gave the Israelis. Even though the Palestinians were a subject people, defenseless and without any defined international status, only they, the victims of the Zionist enterprise, could give the Israelis absolute and final legitimacy. Only Palestinian recognition could liberate them from deep mental anguish, from guilt feelings over the fact that the Zionist enterprise had been achieved by the destruction of the Palestinians. If the Arabs themselves "accept the Zionist enterprise," then they, the Israeli liberals, are liberated from the moral dilemmas that have plagued them during the years of bloody struggle, a struggle that forced on them a painful conflict between patriotic-power values and humanist-universal ones. For this reason the voices of the liberal left, its writers and poets, were euphoric on the day the Madrid conference opened. No diplomatic crisis could rob them of the sense that this was "a historic day, on which the process that will determine eternity began." For this reason they were also sensitive to the Palestinians' longing for legitimacy and entirely content with the procedural and symbolic symmetry created in Madrid.

A peace process in which representatives of the two warring communities participated was, then, the object—a peace process, not necessarily peace terms. This is why it was not important to Yehoshua what peace was achieved: "Peace with the PLO or without the PLO, with Jordan or without Jordan," and so on. For the same reason, Yehoshua could announce, "We are silent now," and tell Israeli Prime Minister Yitzhak Shamir, "Go your own way, with your intrigues. The delegation is all yours. The authority is all yours. But peace will come. Now."

Shamir and the political culture he represented did not attribute to the peace process the moral, metapolitical significance that the left did. The process was forced on him, but good came of it. From his point of view, deliberately dragging out the negotiations was an effective way of putting the status quo on a firm foundation and accelerating the construction of settlements. Shamir did not conduct the process with duplicity; he deceived no one. In the months preceding the Madrid conference, and while bilateral talks were being held in Washington, the Shamir government embarked on a settlement campaign of huge dimensions in the occupied territories. The prime minister's position was not in doubt. He was not willing to exchange territories for peace. If others chose to see this as but an "opening position," that was their problem. The Likud leader attributed no special value to the legitimacy the Arabs were giving Israel; the left's pangs of conscience had never bothered him. He was willing to pay for legitimacy with counterlegitimacy—"peace for peace" rather than "territories for peace." His brutal worldview was compatible with a brutal reality; with his determination, he succeeded in forcing humiliating conditions on the Palestinians. It was no concern of his that these conditions caused a split in their ranks, and that their lack of success brought many of them to the point of despair and instigated a sharp rise in violence in the territories. He trusted to his power to enforce his will. There was no doubt that as long as his political culture ruled Israel, there would be no progress in the peace negotiations; this became clear during the first rounds of the bilateral talks.

The disappointment of the morning after Madrid made a modest contribution to the Likud's defeat in the 1992 elections, although domestic issues were more involved. "For the Israeli public it was important to be involved in the negotiating process, whether or not it was producing results at any given time," one pollster said. As long as the talks continued, optimism grew, and it did not decline despite the lack of movement in the discussions. The Israeli public did not, however, grasp the connection between the peace process and the need to make painful concessions. The pollsters concluded from the public's responses that there was a "creeping dovish trend." It had been discerned as much as ten years earlier, and grew more pronounced in the summer of 1991, "after having halted and even reversed" when the Gulf War broke out.

This conclusion, which the peace movement rushed to claim as "proof of its success," and on which the Americans pinned their optimism about the peace process, was based on the datum "75 percent support the return of territories for peace." An examination of these polls shows that this included all those willing to make "any concession," even a minimal one that would leave small areas without any geopolitical significance in Arab hands. The fact that fewer than 20 percent were prepared to "return most" of the territories did not affect the pollsters' conclusion about the "creeping dovish trend." Nor did the fact that 57 percent wanted the territories annexed and three-quarters advocated refusing to return to the 1967 borders "even in the face of American pressure." Returning territories was thus a dichotomous question—one was either for it or against it—and a person was defined as a "dove" even if he was only willing to return a swatch of desert and favored annexing the rest. That implied that the return of territories was something unilateral—as if the big-hearted Israelis were giving up something that legally belonged to them and the Arabs must accept what they are given, singing the praises of the other side's dovishness. When the Arabs were offered the Allon Plan (which gave them half the territories), not one of them was prepared to discuss it. Twenty-five years later, the willingness to give up a tiny patch of the territories was seen as a victory for the peace movement. The doves pinched themselves and went on living in the illusion that their approach was valid; the right redoubled its efforts to establish facts that would neutralize the risk that "parts of the homeland" would be conceded.

When the melodrama ended, the exhausted actors left the stage. Each delegation returned home, but two of them returned to the same home—to Jerusalem. The Israelis returned to their offices, while the Palestinians returned from the incubator of Madrid to the harsh reality of the occupation, and to the substandard living conditions that had been created during the Intifada. The members of the delegation, who had enjoyed an artificial symmetry between them and their conquerors, were once again subject people whom any soldier could arrest. Those who had sent them, the Palestinian people, whose hopes had soared, petitioned them for help with their troubles. These had grown worse with the wider use of collective punishment. But the members of the delegation could do little. In the eyes of the Israeli government they had no standing.

Members of the Palestinian delegation began drawing up position papers on Palestinian independence and summoned panels of experts to recommend plans of action in all areas, from communications to industrial development. Yet none of this activity had any connection with harsh reality. Between 1988 and 1991, there had been an annual decline of some 20 percent in the territories' GNP; the annual per capita income was $1,400 on the West Bank and $800 in Gaza. As a percentage of the work force, the unemployment rate reached 30–40 percent. Hundreds of millions of dollars that had been sent to the territories by Palestinians employed in Arab countries stopped coming, and after the Gulf War, the aid given to the territories by the Gulf countries, tens of millions of dollars a year, was cut off. Economic hardship, frustration, the lack of progress in the peace talks, the increase in Israel's use of force, and the growing number of Palestinian deaths in the wake of the army's revision of its firing orders led to increasing opposition to the PLO's political line and to growing support for Hamas, which rejected the peace process absolutely. In addition to this, the Palestinian public was exhibiting less and less solidarity and willingness to obey the orders of the Intifada command—commercial strikes were not universally observed, nor was the boycott of Israeli goods.

The troubles even received literary expression. At the beginning of the Intifada, the Palestinian national poet Mahmoud Darwish wrote paeans to his people's victory: "[Israel] your time to go has come / Die where you like but not among us." Four years later he wrote: "Truth has two faces / The black snow is above our city / We can add no despair to our despair." The troubles were a catalyst for acts of terror and knife attacks. During the Likud government's last nine months of power, October 1991–June 1992, 243 people were killed, among them 22 Jews. Seventy-five Palestinians were killed by the security forces and 162 by their own people. The incidence of the use of firearms by Palestinians increased, crossing the red lines drawn by the Intifada during its early years. Israel reacted to this escalation by revising the army's firing orders. It also established army units whose soldiers disguised themselves as Palestinians, penetrated into the heart of Palestinian settlements, and in many cases opened fire indiscriminately. The cycle of violence continued until the eve of the general elections of June 1992. Yet its effect on the elections was different than in the past. If in the past Palestinian violence had strengthened the right, which exploited hatred and fear for its own political purposes, this time the voters

True, the gap between the haves and the have-nots grew, but in contrast with the past, the haves were no longer just members of the established Ashkenazi group. The massive influx of members of the weaker classes into government led to protectionism and inefficient, ineffective, and even corrupt government. Yet it also improved the self-image of large groups and even contributed to the consolidation of a self-confident new elite. One could see this as the consummation of the Likud's historical purpose, and if so, Labor leaders hoped Likud's traditional supporters would be willing to make political choices unencumbered by their feeling, true or false, that they had been disadvantaged.

The Labor party undoubtedly based its hope of returning to power on the calculation that the political and social divides were no longer congruent. Accordingly, it planned to campaign for the support of traditional Likud voters and make it clear that a victory for Labor would not mean radical change. The upheaval of 1992 would not, Labor promised, have the radical social significance of the upheaval of 1977.

The election campaign was prosaic and sober in a way that was hardly in keeping with people's dramatic expectations. It catered to the public's desire to focus on everyday issues such as employment, housing, immigration and absorption, and the extortion practiced by the religious parties, not the fundamental questions of the peace process and withdrawal from the territories. The campaign's professional strategists impressed upon party leaders that they should refrain from accentuating the political contrast between the parties. On the eve of the elections, it was already clear that a two-party system was in the making, but without social and ideological polarization. These trends were indicated by the prevailing mood among population groups that traditionally tended to emphasize issues of ideology and principle—young people voting for the first time, and the Arab voting public.

Tens of thousands of young Jews debated whether to vote for Meretz (the united left block) or Tsomet (a movement with an extreme nationalist-security message that rejects any compromise with the Arabs). These young people, facing army service that would station many of them in the occupied territories for long periods, did not cast their votes on the basis of this fundamental issue. They were thus able to discern a common denominator between two parties at opposite ends of the political spectrum. For them, Meretz's support for the establishment of a Palestinian state on the West Bank and in Gaza and Tsomet's rejection of territorial compromise were irrelevant. Young people tended to vote for these two parties because both were perceived as "clean," untainted by political horse-trading. Both promised to fight the religious coercion that prevented young people from conducting their lives freely. Both parties made impressive gains in the elections.

If prosaic sobriety characterized the voting patterns of ideological minorities, it is hardly surprising that the same sobriety prevailed among the voters of the relatively content Israeli center, which has always been most concerned with the satisfaction of its routine needs. This public wanted a change of government and voted for Yitzhak Rabin because he represented both extremes—he was the minister of defense who had controlled the Arabs with an iron fist, but also a statesman who promised peace in "six to nine months."

During the election campaign, it was already clear that the lead item on the Israeli Arab agenda was not the question of the territories and the future of the peace process, but rather the issue of equal rights. The issues emphasized were discrimination in employment and in the availability of municipal services, inequality of opportunity, and the aspiration for a larger slice of the national pie. The results of the elections in the Arab sector proved that internal Israeli issues had greater weight than Palestinian national issues. The voting showed a strong tendency toward integration into the Israeli political system—for the first time in fifteen years, more Arabs voted for Jewish parties than for Arab ones. While there was a decline in voter turnout, and tens of thousands of votes were wasted because they were cast for Arab parties that did not earn the minimum number of votes required for representation in the Knesset, the eight Arabs elected found themselves in a bargaining position the Israeli Arab community had never before enjoyed. Rabin's narrow "blocking majority" in the Knesset—the majority that made it impossible for the Likud to form a government—depended on the Arab Democratic party of Mohammed Daroushe and the predominantly Arab communists.

These results seemed at first glance to indicate that the "Israeli" component of Israeli Arab identity had taken precedence over the "Palestinian" component. This conclusion is based, however, on an erroneous concept—that the definition of collective identity is determined by modes of political behavior. Such thinking is characteristic of Jewish observers, for whom the world is divided into "good" Arabs and "bad" Arabs. The "good" or "loyal" Arabs are those who vote for Jewish-Zionist parties, while the "bad" Arabs are those who vote for "anti-Zionist" parties, which are at best "nationalist" and at worst "PLO fronts."

The Israeli Arabs had long ago abandoned this simplistic

dichotomy, however; they cast their votes according to objective rather than ideological criteria, to advance their collective interests as much as possible. Israeli electoral politics had become a legitimate arena of Palestinian national endeavor. Israeli Arab voting patterns in the 1992 elections indicated that this community soberly evaluated its position. The peace process had left it on the margins; the status of Israeli Arabs as a national minority in Israel was not under discussion in the negotiations, and neither could they influence the process in any way. It was only natural, then, for them to focus on their problems as citizens of the Jewish state.

Yitzhak Rabin's promise that he would quickly reach an agreement with the Palestinians was weighed against his actions as the minister of defense who had repressed the Intifada with an iron fist. Israeli Arabs reached the conclusion that he might advance the peace process. The weakness of the glue binding the Jewish left and the Israeli Arabs together was demonstrated when Arab support for the left-wing Meretz party actually declined. This happened even though Meretz's positions on the occupied territories and the establishment of a Palestinian state are close to the positions of most Israeli Arabs.

In contrast, there was a dramatic increase in support for an ultra-orthodox Jewish party that had nothing in common with Israeli Arabs, but was the party of the Ministry of the Interior, which provided generous budgets to Arab villages and towns. Since the Arab members of the Knesset as a block had guaranteed Yitzhak Rabin's election to the prime ministership, for the first time in Israel's history, the governing party engaged in formal coalition negotiations with the Arab parties. The prime minister designate promised to take a range of measures to improve the status of the Israeli Arab minority, so acknowledging their status as a group with collective rights. The Arab parties were not invited to participate in the coalition, however, showing that they were still seen as unfit to be full partners in the national decision-making process. Even though the government of the left undertook to make several changes on the municipal level, it continued to toe the traditional line, denying the Israeli Arab minority full legitimacy. The government continued to avoid the question of whether the State of Israel is the state of all its citizens or just the state of the Jewish people, and it continued to endorse institutional discrimination on an ethnic basis.

In contrast to the negligible change in the Israeli Arabs' status within Israel, there was a far-reaching metamorphosis in their relations with the Arab world in general and with the PLO in particular. A few months after the 1992 elections, leaders of the Israeli Arab minority visited King Hussein in Amman. It was an emotional meeting: the king "choked back his tears," and one Jordanian told the guests: "It was a historic error to boycott you; you preserved your culture and honor. You are Arabs even if you are citizens of Israel."

There was an element of poetic justice in the restoration of the Israeli Arabs' lost honor after years of their being treated as traitors, and they were proud and satisfied that their fight had finally been granted recognition. There was, however, an even more dramatic aspect of this metamorphosis. The Israeli Arabs had turned from a group needing legitimacy into one able to grant it. Their position in the Israeli domestic political system allowed them to manifest ever-greater involvement in the Palestinian struggle against the Israeli authorities' severe enforcement measures, and to become a senior factor in the political struggle among the leaders of the PLO. The Arab members of the Knesset pointedly made a public visit to Tunis, where they were received with open arms. Yassir Arafat, whose international prestige had been severely compromised during the Gulf War, wanted the Israeli Arabs' help in his efforts to break the taboo against meetings with the PLO, and to achieve public recognition of his sole authority to engage in bilateral negotiations with Israel. Israel's submissive Arabs gained self-confidence that allowed them to act on the domestic front by virtue of their status as Israeli citizens, and on the external front as an integral part of the Palestinian national movement. There was no contradiction between these two aspects of the struggle—on the contrary, they complemented each other.

The boring election campaign of 1992 was quickly forgotten. The victory of the left was naturally interpreted as that of the political camp aspiring to reconciliation with the Palestinians and willing to make far-reaching concessions to achieve it. Ironically, the ideological dichotomy between the Likud and Labor, played down during the campaign, became the touchstone of their results. Those for whom the problem of the territories was the most important issue facing Israel refused to take the election results simply as an expression of the voters' desire to get rid of a bad government. They had a hard time grasping that what Yitzhak Rabin's victory really signified was that the question of the territories had been stripped of ideology.

In fact, the Rabin government's first actions proclaimed a complete revision of national priorities—an energetic "pursuit of peace," "ongoing talks," "autonomy within a year," and especially "stopping the settlements." The entire world, and the Palestinians first and foremost, believed that a new leaf had been turned over and that the ancient conflict was approaching its end. Israel's international standing instantly improved and the United States, which had not hidden its distaste for the Likud, displayed open sympathy for the Labor government. All this was spurred on by the Israeli government's decisions to cut back construction in the settlements (discussed previously) and by the new instructions given to the delegations to the bilateral talks. The Israeli negotiators were ordered to discuss the real issues and not to waste time scoring points in the public relations duel.

It quickly became clear, however, that the new government's positions were not backed by the requisite energy to lift the negotiations skyward. Rabin clung to the negotiating framework established in Madrid and showed no eagerness to deviate from the Likud's positions. This despite the fact that in opposition, and in its election platform, the Labor party had spoken differently. The Palestinians soon began complaining that the proposals now being put forward by the Israelis were the same ones proposed by the Shamir government, "rewarmed and repackaged." The Palestinians were disappointed because the Rabin government's rhetoric had led them to believe that on the central issue in the negotiations, the "interim agreement," there was no real disagreement in principle. The Palestinians saw the negotiations as a linear process. For them, the interim stage was one step in the process of carrying out UN Security Council Resolution 242, and they believed that it would lead directly into the final stage in which they would be able to realize their right to self-determination. This position was diametrically opposed to the Likud's stance.

The autonomy plan initiated by Menachem Begin that was included in the Camp David accords was for the Likud a permanent solution to the problem of the occupied territories. It was meant to establish "autonomy for people" rather than an autonomous region with defined geographic borders; its authority was limited to the personal and administrative, and it lacked any reference to self-determination. According to the Likud, the interim arrangement was to be established in such a way that there was no contradiction between it and a final stage that was simply the continuation of the status quo (whether this took the form of full annexation to Israel or a continuation of creeping annexation). There was no way to bridge the gulf between the positions of the Likud and the Palestinians, so there was no progress in the talks. Now, facing a new partner that had declared its willingness for "territorial compromise on all fronts," the Palestinians believed they would make progress.

As the Palestinians understood it, the new Israeli government considered Israeli rule over a considerable part of the territories to be temporary, to be terminated at the end of the peace process. Autonomy or self-government based on this conception of the permanent solution is not like autonomy based on an aspiration to perpetuate Israeli control over the territories. It is a stage that prepares the way for a geopolitical division that involves the creation of two separate governmental systems. While the question of the boundaries of the territorial compromise remained to be resolved, there was an opening for a concrete discussion of the authority to be granted to the Palestinians, with every area of authority so transferred containing within it the kernel of the permanent arrangement.

What in fact took place, however, was a discussion along the lines of the Likud-mandated agenda. The Rabin government refused to link the interim agreement with the final arrangement, or even to make any clear statement about the autonomy's significance in the context of a territorial compromise. This it justified by invoking a formality—that the permanent status of the territories was to be discussed only after the establishment of the self-governing entity.

Its inability to define for itself its conception of the territories' permanent status in a way that could serve as a basis for drawing up the interim agreements showed that the Rabin government suffered from internal contradictions that the Likud and the Palestinians did not have. Their positions were internally consistent—antithetic, but solid. The lack of internal logic was also discernible in the specific discussions of the "territorial dimension"—the question of the territorial jurisdiction of the self-governing entity.

The Likud government had refused to define geographical boundaries; the Labor government, however, did not feel itself bound by this taboo. Many thought that an impasse had been overcome and a breakthrough achieved. It soon became clear, however, that the Rabin government had no intention of basing the boundaries of the Palestinian autonomous entity's jurisdiction on its conception of territorial compromise, whether in accordance with the Allon Plan or any other geopolitical scheme. It wished, instead, to define autonomy (outside the Gaza Strip) at the municipal level. According to the Israeli government's proposals, the autonomous entity's authority was to apply to the municipal boundaries of Palestinian cities, towns, and villages—that is, to no more than 7 percent of the area of the West Bank. These were bits of land scattered all over the region, and no individual area was larger than a few thousand acres.

Their isolation from one another, and the fact that most of

the West Bank's physical infrastructure was outside them, meant that such boundaries for the Palestinian autonomous authority were a joke. Moreover, Israel conditioned its consent to these absurd borders on the proviso that the Israeli settlements also receive "autonomous areas of authority" of similar dimensions to that inhabited by a million Palestinians. This meant, in short, that the Palestinians were expected to grant legitimacy to the allocation of huge areas on which hundreds of thousands of additional Jews could be settled. The upshot of this was that the negotiations remained stuck exactly where they had been in 1981 during the Camp David autonomy negotiations with the Egyptians and the Americans, which were boycotted by the Palestinians. The specific and complex discussions of land, water rights, powers and responsibilities that took place were disguised as rational and pragmatic, but in fact the agenda was simply a cover for the hidden real agenda, where absolute values clashed.

Two years of fruitless discussions made it clear to anyone who was prepared to see that the Israeli-Palestinian dialogue remained stuck in its pre-substantial phase. The lack of progress in the negotiations with the Palestinians led many to conclude that the breakthrough would come in the negotiations with Syria. But there the tables were turned. Whereas in the negotiations with the Palestinians, Israel refused to link the interim stage to the final agreement, in the negotiations over the Golan Heights, it was Israel that demanded that arrangements for a permanent peace in all its particulars be concluded as a precondition for its willingness to discuss arrangements for withdrawal from the disputed territories. The Syrians took the opposite position.

The deadlock created an urgent need to prove, at any price, that progress was being made—and only in the negotiations with

Jordan could any progress be pointed to. This was not a revival of the old "Jordanian option"; rather, it was bilateral discussion of matters such as the precise location of the desert border between the two countries. In their desire to show progress at any price, Israeli spokesmen fudged the fundamental difference between the secret talks Israeli representatives had conducted with King Hussein over the previous twenty-five years and the negotiations being conducted in the framework of the peace process. The discussions held before the Madrid conference did not deal with bilateral issues, but rather with active Jordanian involvement on the West Bank and in Gaza. Israel then proposed four alternatives: territorial compromise on the basis of the Allon Plan; a framework leading to territorial compromise by stages; a functional compromise, according to which the Jordanians would assume administrative responsibility for the territories, while Israel remained responsible for security; and a permanent condominium. There were those who argued that these negotiations were hopeless from the start, while others claimed that political constraints and lack of nerve frustrated them. Still others maintained that the Jordanian option was entirely a pipe dream of the labor movement, which wished to externalize the Palestinian problem in order to avoid unresolvable ideological and moral dilemmas.

The Intifada put an end to the illusion of the Jordanian option. King Hussein detached himself from the West Bank and Gaza Strip, and only a Palestinian option remained. But the impasse in the pursuit of this option also prevented the institutionalization of the de facto peace between Israel and Jordan, because the fates of Jordanians, Palestinians, and Israelis were all interwoven. Two generations of conflict could not be resolved through bilateral agreement that did not address the problem of the Palestinian refugees in Jordan, the citizenship of the inhabitants of the occupied territories, the division of the water resources of the Jordan basin, and economic relationships between the two banks.

The peace process began with the spectacular show in the king of Spain's palace and gave up the ghost in the summer of 1993, after having been on a respirator for more than a year. Even though only two years had passed since the Gulf War was supposed to have instated a new order, institutionalized by the Madrid conference, the international reality of 1993 in the Middle East belonged to another era. The Madrid conference had been nothing but a show, put on for internal American political purposes. Its participants had been dragged to it against their wills, or after they had made sure in advance that it would not lead anywhere. With the exit of President Bush and Secretary of State Baker and the entry onto the scene of President Clinton, the situation changed entirely. The former had needed a peace process to justify their presumption and boasts during the war and thereafter, whereas the latter had no mandate to serve as a policeman enforcing a Pax Americana. His administration was manifestly unable to cope with internal ethnic conflicts such as those in Bosnia-Herzegovina, Somalia, and Rwanda.

Despite this, no one dared pull the plug on the respirator and officially announce the death of the Madrid process. All those involved wanted it to continue, not because it would produce results, but because each party, especially the Israelis and the Palestinians, had an egotistical interest in it. The continuation of the process was essential for the Palestinians, because the diplomatic negotiations were the only international forum in which they participated as players of equal status. Terminating the process would have robbed them of a platform for stating their positions and presenting their plight.

The continuation of the Madrid process was also vital to the Rabin government, which had come to power on the basis of a self-proclaimed "clear mandate for peace," declaring all the while that a political settlement was within reach. Acknowledging failure would have extinguished the raison d'être of the self-styled "peace government," which cited the need to make progress in the peace process both as an excuse for all its failures and to justify collective punishment measures in the territories. These, the government insisted, were necessary for the success of, or secondary to the requirements of, this one-time opportunity of achieving peace.

The continuation of the pretense of a peace process had allowed the Rabin government to act out a contradiction—negotiations were being conducted but were divorced from the reality in the field. Flexible rhetoric coexisted with harsh enforcement measures in the territories. As the Rabin government saw it, taking a flexible line in the negotiations and using force to establish facts in the field were not contradictory but mutually reinforcing. The reasoning was that tough measures in the territories lowered the level of violence and created an atmosphere more conducive to the peace process. This rationale was cited chiefly by Labor's partners in the coalition, the members of Meretz. Until joining Rabin's government they had been sharp critics of the iron fist in the occupied territories; now they found themselves having to argue in favor of collective punishment. All things considered, this dichotomy was a comfortable one for the Rabin government: the better it managed to foster its peacemaking image, the bolder it became in pursuing a policy of force. No one, after all, would have dared to accuse it of sabotaging an opportunity for peace. Could a Likud government do better?

In the polluted field conditions of the Gaza Strip and the West Bank, life became harsher in a way unseen by eyes blinded by the bilateral talks. Red lines drawn at the beginning of the Intifada were crossed. There were mass deportations, homes were shelled with missiles, a closure severed the territories from Israel. These actions raised the violence of the confrontation to a new level. Yet this quantum leap did not disturb the sleep of the Israeli consensus. When the Palestinians came to U.S. Secretary of State Warren Christopher and presented their protests about the situation in the territories, he responded: "How long will you go on complaining? The time has come to start talking business!" In other words, talk to me in the jargon I know and don't bother me with the street talk of reality.

In the middle of December 1992, in direct response to the kidnapping and murder of a Border Guard policeman, Nissim Toledano, 415 Palestinian men accused of being leaders of Hamas on the West Bank and in the Gaza Strip were deported to Lebanon. The significance of this deportation resembles that of a Japanese haiku—it is a microcosm that contains an entire world. When the outer layer of rhetoric and the sequence of events leading up to it are peeled away, what remains is a kernel of concepts and emotions as old as the Jewish-Arab conflict, the components of which have not changed since it was born a century ago.

A single violent event, following on a whole series of serious and humiliating incidents in which Jewish blood was spilled, was thus sufficient to reinvoke the feeling among Israelis that the hostility of the Arabs is a natural trait, which can be confronted only with force. The wave of murders committed by Hamas dictated a forceful response, which was itself nothing more than the repetition of an ancient ritual—the deportation of the enemy.

The deportation in turn summoned up the Palestinians' ancient trauma—the trauma of being uprooted and exiled, incurred in the 1930s and especially during the 1947–49 war. The refugee camp built by the deportees in the snowy Lebanese mountains even looked exactly like one of the Palestinian camps set up after the Palestinian tragedy of 1948. The opening scene of the deportation thus greatly resembled the first act of a "Settlement and Self-Defense" pageant of the kind staged in Jewish schools, and also a performance of Palestinian ethnic folklore in an East Jerusalem theater. Both have the same effect—they create an almost absolute tribal solidarity, blurring the differences between left and right, between nationalists and fundamentalists.

Trusting to their physical advantage and believing, as in the past, that military measures could compel the enemy to come to terms with the status quo, the Israelis sought to wipe out Palestinian hostility by force. But against all logic, the Palestinian community refused to submit to the dictates of power, robbing the Israelis of the hope that force would buy them tranquility. Each side exploited its relative advantage—the Israelis used their military might, and the Palestinians used international public opinion, the weapon of the weak. The tie that resulted left the new-old problem unsolved, while the photogenic suffering of the deported Palestinians underlined the arbitrariness of the use of force.

The deportation, which earned the epithet "mini-transfer," did not lower the level of violence. Quite the opposite—Hamas's daring increased, and the following spring fifteen Israelis were murdered in a single month. In March 1993, when two policemen were killed near Hadera, in the heart of Israel, the government made the strategic decision to impose a "closure" of the occupied territories, sealing them off from Israel. This was not the first time that extreme measures had been taken to separate the occupied territories from Israel proper, and the severity of the measures adopted was directly proportional to the intensification of Palestinian violence, and especially to the murders committed in the heart of Israel.

The greatest efforts were put into restricting the movement of Palestinians into Jewish zones; individual entry permits were required, first in Gaza and then on the West Bank. The separation reached its height when the Gulf War broke out and two million Palestinians were put under closure and entirely forbidden to enter Jewish areas. After forty-five days, during which the Palestinians exhausted their food supplies, the general curfew was lifted and a pass system was instituted, one that was very similar to that used in South Africa at the height of apartheid. Palestinians were allowed to enter Jewish zones only to work, only during daylight, and only if they had a formal referral to a specific place of work. Their employer had to pick them up from one of the checkpoints in a vehicle with a yellow Israeli license plate and return them in the evenings. Palestinians were allowed to work only in agriculture and construction. "Whoever comes here to work has to be at his workplace until work ends and then return to his home. There is one single rule for any resident of the territories seen walking through the streets of Tel Aviv—to be frisked by the police and arrested if he has violated the law," declared the Tel Aviv chief of police.

Since every Arab was prima facie suspect of being in Israel without a permit, everyone who looked "oriental" suffered. This established an ethnic classification on a manifestly genetic basis. The complex and computerized pass system (Arabs permitted to enter Israel were given magnetic cards) could not, however, defeat market forces. The Jewish economy was hungry for Palestinians prepared to do hard physical labor for low pay and to work at jobs considered odious by Jewish workers. Many Jewish employers helped Palestinians evade the closure. In March 1993, just before the imposition of the "closure without a time limit," some 120,000 Palestinians were working in Israel, 50,000 of them without permits.

The enforced separation imposed by the Rabin government was different to those implemented by its predecessors. The government declared that the situation "would never again [be] as it was." The army set up more than a hundred checkpoints along the Green Line and prevented the entry of Palestinians into Israel, including East Jerusalem. The military administration revoked all work permits; merchants wishing to do business in Israel and people in need of medical care were sent home. The cabinet charged a committee chaired by the minister of labor with the preparation of a program to ensure that Israel could live with the separation permanently.

The hunger for cheap manpower forced the government to import tens of thousands of foreign workers, from Romania, Thailand, and the Philippines. Thai workers watered plants in the greenhouses of Israeli farms bordering Gaza while 40 percent of Gaza's labor force remained unemployed. The closure soon changed from a security measure to a far-reaching political reality, with implications for all areas of life, especially on the psychological and social levels. Separation from the Palestinians was meant to define once more the psychological borders within which Israeli citizens could feel safe. In other words, it was meant to fence off anxiety geophysically.

The decision also had an ideological and nostalgic component. The separation from the Palestinians was meant to recreate the bygone, innocent days of "little Israel," the pre-1967 Israel, when the conflict was external and simple rather than chronic, endemic, and intercommunal. The government emphasized a return to the supreme Zionist value of "Hebrew labor," which had made it possible for an independent Jewish society and economy to develop into a foundation for the Jewish state. Having set the boundaries of "little Israel," the government wished to reorganize the violent confrontation in frameworks similar to those of a conventional war. The closure defined the battlefield—the occupied territories. In these areas, the government ruled, "the army may act to its fullest ability in accordance with its own considerations, and there is no political constraint on the army within the framework of the law." The rules of engagement were revised to allow soldiers to shoot to kill any "armed" man, including those armed with Molotov cocktails and cement blocks. There were ministers who proposed using tanks and aircraft in the territories, and while these proposals were rejected, the wartime mood prevailed, and the government enjoyed broad public support for the steps it was taking.

The closure regime and the separation were supported by right, left, and center, with each political bloc justifying it in accordance with its ideological position. For the left, geographic separation was a means toward the establishment of an independent Palestinian entity, while for the right it was a means of suppressing the Arabs. "The Arabs have no reason to be among us," went the talk on the streets of Israeli cities. "Just as the Jews have stopped eating shishkebab in Ramallah, the Arabs also have to get used to living separately. Isn't that what they want?" This perception of symmetry is perhaps comprehensible as a simplistic reaction, but when senior politicians said the same thing, it was merely cynical. Rulers need their subject peoples only for services, while subject peoples are dependent on their rulers for everything.

Not surprisingly, the separation was accomplished entirely at the expense of the Palestinians. It was a unilateral system that applied only to the subject population, exclusively in furtherance of the ruling community's interests. So long as the ruling community held an absolute monopoly on power and on enforcement mechanisms, the separation could be implemented flexibly, changing as the rulers' interests changed. Several ministers repeatedly demanded that the government "release funding for infrastructure development programs in the territories and massively increase Israeli and international investments in the territories." In practice, however, only small sums were allocated, for the establishment of make-work schemes on a small scale. The ministers who demanded increased investment in the territories knew full well that the sums needed to make the territories economically independent amounted to billions of dollars over a period of fifteen years.

The closure began to melt away as a result of pressures from Israeli employers. The greatest pressure came, not unexpectedly, from construction and agriculture, where work had ground almost completely to a halt. The number of Palestinian laborers receiving "special permits" grew ever larger, but hundreds of thousands remained unemployed. The laborers who had lost their livelihoods did not receive unemployment compensation, even though most of them had worked in Israel for many years and had had national insurance payments deducted from their paychecks. According to computations by Palestinian economists, the economic loss to the inhabitants of the occupied territories was about $100 million a month, two-thirds of that from the loss of work in Israel (which until the closure had accounted for a third of the territories' GNP).

An economy already depressed after five years of Intifada slowed even more. While Palestinians were not going hungry, tens of thousands were living at a subsistence level, and hundreds of thousands had to eat up their savings. The boasts of Palestinian spokesmen about the "establishment of an independent economic infrastructure" were proven hollow. The ongoing misery of the Palestinians was a daily slap in the face to Israeli liberals, who had believed wholeheartedly that the separation was not only a political move that would advance the cause of peace but also a morally correct one. When the closure became an end rather than a means and was institutionalized conceptually (even if in practice it could not be fully implemented), Israel came dangerously close to the bantustan model of South Africa. The ideological justification was also similar—the "liberal" *verligtes* in the ruling South African National party believed that they were creating a system of separation between ethnic groups that would allow each group to obtain political rights and benefit from economic opportunities in its own region. The openly racist *verkramptes* saw apartheid as a way of preserving themselves and their civilization from the "savages."

The closure's effect on the peace process was immediate, and it focused on Jerusalem. East Jerusalem, which in the eyes of Israelis is an inseparable part of their sovereign state, was severed from its hinterland. This denied tens of thousands of Palestinians access to their major urban center. It also cut the northern West Bank off from the southern West Bank, an intolerable state of affairs. In addition to creating human suffering, it brought the problem of Jerusalem to the fore. Continuing negotiations while Jerusalem was cut off would be tantamount to the Palestinians' surrendering East Jerusalem, the heart of their national aspirations, to Israel. The Palestinians demanded of the Israelis and the Americans that Jerusalem's status be clarified immediately. This most complex of problems, which both sides had previously agreed to put off for as long as possible, thus became central. The ship of the negotiations hit the rocky reef of Jerusalem. The Israelis accused the Palestinians of having raised the issue of Jerusalem intentionally in order to sabotage the talks, while the Palestinians accused the Israelis of an attempt to grab Jerusalem by force.

The mass deportation and the closure were not arbitrary measures. They were classic solutions to the problem of continuing intercommunal violence. There was a great temptation to solve the problem with quick and drastic surgery. What could be nicer than to wake up in the morning and realize that the problem had been solved—that the "others" had disappeared? The sense of there being no way out, of the situation's continuing day in and day out, the continuing violence, the anxiety, and the lack of fundamental security, led to the feeling that radical surgery was necessary. The festering limb must be amputated to prevent the gangrene from spreading to the rest of the body. Each side dreamt of the other side's disappearance. If it could not disappear physically, perhaps it could at least be distanced. If it could not be exterminated or deported, perhaps it could at least be eliminated from one's consciousness, conceptually externalized. The poet Mahmoud Darwish urged the Israelis: "Leave our land." Israeli rabbis declared that the Arabs were the biblical tribe of Amalek, whom God had commanded the Jews to destroy utterly. An Israeli leader known for his moderate positions declared more than once: "I would also like the Arabs to vanish from Jerusalem, but what can we do if they do not oblige?"

Radical solutions require radical measures, involving an unrestrained use of physical force. Each side knows that the other side can be made to disappear only through use of cruel measures enforced by military superiority. Even people and groups that have no compunctions about the brutal use of power need to rationalize it, which is done via the psychological defense mechanism known as projection. Each side projects its own violent destructive urge on the other and believes that extermination is the enemy's real goal. That being the case, the precept "rise earlier to kill the man who is coming to kill you" is a legitimate guide to action. The psychological need to project violent urges on the other side, there to be "discovered," does not make the danger of extermination into mere unfounded paranoia, just as it does not necessarily make it into an actual threat. The shouts of "Death to the Arabs" and "Slaughter the Jews" heard in every serious confrontation are the crude verbal expressions of these urges. They are the compost fertilizing ideas and actions that actually aspire to cause the other side's disappearance. The radical elimination of intercommunal polarity can take many forms, among them physical destruction, forceful expulsion, spatial separation, political separation, and assimilation.

"What is the difference between South Africa, Northern Ireland, and Israel on the one hand and New England and Australia on the other?" a cynic asked. His answer: "In New England and Australia, most of the natives no longer exist—they were exterminated." This is one way of putting an end to intercommunal conflicts. In fact, the methodical extermination of native populations was once an accepted means of resolving conflicts between immigrant and native societies, creating, ex post facto, a homogeneous society and a "nation-state." In the nineteenth century, planned genocide carried out by governments (in contrast to pogroms and mass murders committed by groups and individuals) came to be considered immoral by the international community, and countries committing such acts placed themselves outside the family of civilized nations. Even after it became illegitimate, genocide was perpetrated in the twentieth century, most infamously the murder of the Armenians by Ottoman Turkey before and during World War I and the Holocaust of European Jewry during World War II. Less well known genocides were committed by the Khmer Rouge in Cambodia, by the Ba'ath regime in Iraq (against the Kurds), and the Hutu and Tutsi peoples of Burundi and Rwanda.

The difference between genocide and population transfer is not particularly clear. The genocides committed against the Armenians and Jews were disguised as "evacuation and emigration." The Germans, who harnessed modern science and technology to their diabolical plot, alone could methodically murder millions of human beings. Other countries and ruling ethnic groups made do with more primitive methods, the most common being uprooting entire populations from their native lands and transporting them under horrible conditions to remote or inhospitable locations. The ethnic map of the world has to a great extent been determined by the forced movement of populations. The course of history and the fate of continents and countries has been affected by the use of expulsion as a means of eliminating intercommunal friction.

There is certainly no space here to enumerate the waves of population transfers that human history has seen. The most notable are the repeated expulsions of the Jewish people, from the deportation of the inhabitants of the kingdom of Israel by the Assyrians through the Spanish expulsion; the expulsion of hundreds of thousands of Protestants, Muslims, and Catholics in Europe in the sixteenth and seventeenth centuries; the forced transfer of the Native Americans in the mid-nineteenth century; the mutual expulsions of Hindus and Muslims in India in 1947–48; the expulsion of the Palestinians from Israel in 1947–48; the expulsions of Germans, Hungarians, and other national minorities during and after World War II; the expulsions of Tartars, Chechins, and Kalmuks from their native areas in the Soviet Union; the transfer of Turks and Greeks in Asia Minor and the Balkans in the years 1914–23, and in Cyprus in 1974; the expulsion of Asians from Uganda in 1982, and of the Chinese from Indonesia in the 1960s; the expulsion of Tamils from Sri Lanka in 1974; the "ethnic cleansing" of the states that emerged from what was formerly Yugoslavia; and the Rwanda tragedy.

The expulsion of communities from their homelands is, like genocide, considered to be an act that runs counter to the fundamental values of civilized society. The International Declaration of Human Rights, signed in 1948, and other international covenants (including the Fourth Geneva Convention of 1949 and onward) forbid expulsions, population transfers, resettlement, and forced relocation of any type.

Those who see population transfer as a legitimate means of ending intercommunal conflicts cite population exchanges that were the product of international agreement. These examples prove, they claim, that the consensual resettlement of populations is legitimate. In fact, only in two instances have governments signed agreements on the mutual exchange of minority populations and their absorption in states where the transferred ethnic group is in the majority. Such agreements were concluded by Turkey and Greece in 1923, involving 2.5 million people, and between Sri Lanka and India in 1964 and 1974, involving about 600,000 people.

The convention signed by the Greeks and Turks in 1923, which ostensibly granted international legitimacy to population transfer as a radical solution to intercommunal frictions, was really nothing but a sleight of hand. The agreement of the two countries involved, and the confirmation of the League of Nations, were exceptions that were never considered to be part of international legal or moral norms. "Voluntary population transfer" is an option that does not exist. It is a bankrupt attempt to grant an aura of respectability to violent acts that border on genocide.

The expulsion of a population in the modern age is generally a result of interstate or civil war. In general, it has been the by-product of hostile acts and has begun spontaneously. Civilians who have been hurt, or who have felt themselves in danger, have left their homes and sought refuge in safe places. Most of those who left believed that their move was temporary. Governments and ethnic leaderships have exploited the panic to launch campaigns of fear and expulsion. This was the character of the population transfers after the partition of India (1947) and the partition of Palestine (1948). On the Indian subcontinent, 14 million people left their homes to move from India to Pakistan or the reverse. More than 700,000 Palestinians became refugees. This kind of population transfer has never brought intercommunal conflicts to an end; it has only changed their form. Among the deportees, the experience of expulsion has added yet another layer to established ancient hatreds and has led to a deep-seated desire for revenge. The deportees, whether they were taken in by their compatriots in "their country" or excluded from the political and social system, constituted an incendiary element that pressured the government to hold fast to its confrontational stance against the neighboring country from which they were exiled. In this way intercommunal conflicts have become part of international conflicts. Germans expelled from eastern Europe, and Hindu, Muslim, Palestinian, Tamil, Hungarian, Albanian, Somali, Greek, and Turkish deportees have all joined militant and radical groups whose goal it is to prevent good relations with the country from which they were expelled.

The disappearance of the "others" has helped the majority community redefine the character of the conflict. The conflict is "externalized," transformed into a foreign country's threat to the territorial integrity, and even existence, of the nation-state. The expelling country views the exiled community as a group of war-mongering refugees trying to sabotage peaceful coexistence between neighboring countries. Transferring the conflict to the interstate level makes it "sterile." Gone are the complex and emotional intercommunal problems; they are replaced by an "international conflict" between abstract bodies "represented" by diplomats and generals. The conflict over a field or a cemetery, over the name of a town and the language to be spoken, become threats to "sovereignty" and to "secure and recognized borders." Population transfer is thus not an attempt to solve the intercommunal struggle, but rather a violent act that has only made a solution even more difficult to achieve.

Population transfer as a way of terminating the Jewish-Arab conflict is a theme that runs straight through the history of the struggle for the land between the Jordan and the sea. The idea has much occupied the Jews because this radical solution has seemed to provide an answer to their aspiration that their community turn instantly from a minority into a majority. Population transfer has been raised in various forms, but entered the political agenda only in the 1930s. It was only natural that political discussion of the issue was connected with the recommendations of the Peel Commission on the partition of Palestine (1936), involving the establishment of a Jewish state in the coastal valley. The commission recommended the voluntary or mandatory transfer of most or all of the Arab population living in the area assigned to the Jewish state. Those who favored partition, led by Ben-Gurion, supported a mandatory or voluntary transfer so long as it enjoyed international (and especially British) acquiescence, was implemented in an orderly fashion, and followed payment of compensation that would allow the resettlement of the exiles in the Arab state to be established alongside the Jewish state. Of course, this partition was never realized, but the population transfer idea did not die. Prior to the United Nations partition resolution of November 1947, the leaders of the Yishuv once again discussed the idea, but made no operative decisions.

At first, the Palestinian community did not consider population transfer as a means of resolving the conflict. It did not need to, since it was the majority in Palestine. Only when there was a reversal of this majority and the Palestinians became a minority, did they draft their own transfer plan. The Palestinian Covenant states that every Jew who immigrated to Palestine after the beginning of the Zionist enterprise will have to leave. Population transfer is thus a by-product of demographic and political circumstances, not an idea on which either side has a monopoly. During the 1947–49 war, the Israeli army forced a large-scale transfer of Arabs. According to Benny Morris's *The Birth of the Palestinian Refugee Problem, 1947–1949* (Cambridge: Cambridge University Press, 1987), the Palestinian Arabs' flight from the areas conquered by the Israelis was in some cases spontaneous and in some cases initiated by the victors. This complex subject is beyond the scope of this book, but in any case, even if these expulsions were not coercive and intentional, the results were those of an a posteriori population transfer. Both the Arabs who left of their own volition and the Arabs who were expelled were forbidden to return to areas within the State of Israel. Many of those who remained were expelled from their homes and resettled elsewhere in Israel. The population transfer of 1947–49 did not win international legitimacy; on the contrary, the problem of the Arab refugees and their right to return to their homes has remained on the international agenda from then until now. Furthermore, nothing was done to compensate the refugees for property they left behind.

In 1967, there was another population transfer, although smaller than that of 1947–49. About 250,000 of the refugees from 1948 who resided in refugee camps in the territories, where they had lived for twenty years, left of their own volition. At the end of the 1967 war, there were attempts to implement a forced population transfer. Residents of cities and villages in areas near the cease-fire line were expelled from their homes and their communities destroyed; the Israeli authorities offered financial "incentives" and free transportation to Palestinians willing to leave; and refugees from the Gaza area were transferred to camps in the Jordan Valley. These attempts to carry out a forced or voluntary population transfer failed, however, and the Palestinians stayed put.

Population transfer as a miracle panacea for the Jewish-Arab conflict never disappeared from the public agenda, and in the 1980s the Moledet (Homeland) party, whose platform centers on "voluntary population transfer," won two seats in the Knesset. The Moledet party was brought into the Likud coalition in 1991, and increased its Knesset representation to three seats in the 1992 elections. Opinion polls have consistently shown that a large portion of the Israeli population accepts transfer of Arabs out of Israel as a legitimate policy option. Despite this, there can be no doubt that the actual implementation of a mass population transfer (as opposed to theoretical discussion) is unacceptable to the leaders of all the political parties in Israel. A few of them (on the right) have been willing to debate the moral and human aspects of the policy but know that as a solution it is "impractical"; others (including leaders of the Likud) consider the idea "political pollution."

Population transfer would seem to be an act that plainly contradicts Israel's image of itself as a Western society committed to democratic, humanist, liberal principles. Those who have found the idea repugnant consider themselves enlightened, and as such they have felt free to preach a more humane alternative—separation of the two populations. After the Gulf War, the Meretz leader Yossi Sarid said: "The more hellish the situation becomes, the more we are faced with either of two alternatives: transfer or separation. If we do not present the separation option rationally, only one option will remain." The intolerability of the intercommunal conflict created a need to end it by erecting an impregnable barrier between the two opponents.

Spatial separation of ethnic groups is a common phenomenon in divided societies. The extent of this separation is a clear measure of the intensity of the conflict. Any real or imagined increase in tension intensifies spatial separation; a decline in tension increases mixing between ethnic groups. People aspire to create a homogeneous ethnic space because separation gives a sense of physical security, reduces friction, and preserves the community's ethnic identity. Spatial separation is important emotionally, since control of a defined territory, even in the local urban or regional context, is of national-emotional value. The preservation of the ethnic purity of one's territory in the face of foreigners grows out of the basic human need for an identity. This is expressed externally with flags, architectural styles and forms, and graffiti. Ethnically homogeneous physical spaces are created naturally. The desire to live close to common community and religious institutions—such as schools, houses of worship, welfare organizations, and social and cultural meeting places, the need for stores where one may purchase the food one is accustomed to, and the sense of security provided by the camaraderie of members of one's own community all create a natural instinct for ethnic segregation. When times are quiet, the elements of distinct ethnic identities become blurred, and elements that divide people according to their economic standing or "modern" lifestyles become stronger. But at times of intercommunal tension, especially when it deteriorates into a violent confrontation, ethnic differences again become acute, and population relocations occur as people return to live behind the ethnic fault line. Some of these moves are spontaneous, but generally they are caused by intimidation. An atmosphere of fear blurs the distinction between unfounded rumors and real acts of violence, and each side huddles together within its homogeneous territory. The fault line itself becomes an area of confrontation, and space becomes a mosaic of alienated islands. Functional and social interactions become restricted to the minimum necessary for daily survival.

Voluntary spatial separation and spatial separation resulting from sporadic acts of violence by extremist groups are most notable in urban spaces, where high population density naturally causes excess friction. Externally, this urban segregation receives concrete and even dramatic expression, since the fault line sometimes runs along alleys no more than two or three yards wide. However, ethnically homogeneous spaces may encompass large areas and even large territories. There is no need to give examples of the phenomenon of ethnic concentration in bi- or poly-ethnic countries, since this is the form of settlement everywhere. There can be no doubt that ethnically segregated spaces contribute to the reduction of tension, the preservation of community identities, and the augmentation of physical and psychological security. Under conditions of severe intercommunal conflict, spatial separation may even be the cornerstone of tolerable relations between the communities, since it guarantees the fundamental interests of both sides by granting a minimum of security, and thus facilitates conflict management.

Zionism, the Jewish people's national liberation movement, aimed to create a new society in the Land of Israel—a distinct and self-sufficient Jewish society. This society developed, consciously and intentionally, almost without establishing connections with the Palestinians. The Zionists aspired to create a separate sociopolitical system, not to turn into a dominant class ruling over and exploiting the natives. Noble ideology went in tandem with a sense of European superiority. It looked down on the natives—on their technological abilities, on their culture, and on their political behavior. The sense that the Jews should be "a people that shall dwell alone" was also fostered by the experience of two thousand years of exile and the bloodily enforced separation that had been the lot of the Jews in other countries.

The Jewish-gentile dichotomy was transferred to Israel and became the emotional infrastructure of the voluntary isolation created by the Jewish community in all spheres of life in Mandatory Palestine—geographic, economic, social, political, and military. The Yishuv's success in making itself into an independent and isolated community made the ideology of separation into an unchallengeable mythology. In fact, it was only this strategy that could have brought the Jews victory in the intercommunal conflict; it was, actually, a necessary response to the uncompromising policy and violent acts of the Palestinian Arabs. During the Arab rebellion of 1936–39, the dual Jewish-Arab society was firmly established and the points of contact between the two sides of the ethnic fault line were reduced to a minimum. Separation received its most extreme expression—population transfer—in the 1947–49 war. When the Jewish state was established, it imposed a regime of functional separation between Jews and Arabs. The Arabs became citizens of the new country, but they had no access to the regime's decision-making centers. They were discriminated against economically and institutionally, in the allocation of material resources, and in the provision of their cultural, education, and symbolic needs—discrimination based on legal classification by birth as members of the Arab minority.

The Six-Day War opened a new era in relations between the Jewish and Arab communities and led to the development of a new type of imposed separation. Legal separation was achieved automatically—the residents of the occupied territories were citizens of a foreign country (on the West Bank) or stateless (in the Gaza Strip). Spatial separation was also the direct outcome of the territories' occupied status. Nothing remained but to establish a functional (economic) separation and, especially, to control the movement of people. In this regard, the government used both separation and integration—separation and discrimination when it came to the Palestinian population and integration in everything that touched on Israeli interests. The Palestinians were not allowed to sell their produce in Israeli markets. Restrictions were placed on when and how residents of the territories might stay in Israel, but there were no restrictions on the movement of Israeli citizens or their presence in the territories. Quite the opposite—the government encouraged Israeli settlement in the heart of Palestinian areas, turning the geographic dividing line (the Green Line) into a division between types of persons and their communities. Israeli citizens carried the Israeli system with them to their settlements in the territories, while their neighbors on the other side of a barbed-wire fence remained outside the system and discriminated against. During the occupation's first twenty years, the model was one of individual integration accompanied by communal segregation. At first, the residents of the

CHAPTER SIX

BREAKTHROUGH

I t is generally accepted that a conflict is ripe for a solution when both parties reach two conclusions: it is impossible to defeat or subdue the enemy by force; and the status quo is intolerable—its cost is greater than the price of compromise. The problem is that it is difficult, if not impossible, to predict the "ripening point." Apparently, the ripening process can be discerned only in retrospect. Historians tend to speak about events that lead to the successful resolution of a conflict as an inevitable process, yet they cannot formulate a theory that explains why some bitter conflicts were resolved just at the point when conditions could not have deteriorated further, while others were ripe for a solution only after improvement of relations created an atmosphere conducive to amicable resolutions.

The Israeli-Palestinian conflict did not seem ripe for a solution in the summer of 1993. Harsh measures taken by the Israeli government in the territories canceled out flexibility in the peace negotiations. Mass deportations, killings by death squads, and stabbing of innocent civilians raised the confrontation to a new level. Israeli representatives in the bilateral talks rehashed old formulas, and Chairman Arafat torpedoed all progress by giving contradictory instructions to Palestinian delegates. The Madrid process was dead, and a pessimistic mood prevailed in Israel and among the Palestinians. Persistent rumors about secret negotiations in a European country were dismissed as propaganda, disseminated by an Israeli government that had promised peace in six or nine months and could not deliver. The PLO sank to its lowest ebb ever. The disintegration of the Soviet Union and the consequences of joining Saddam Hussein left Arafat with empty coffers and political isolation. Almost six years of Intifada had exhausted the population in the occupied territories, the tension between the Palestinian "inside" and the Tunis-based leadership mounted, internal opposition intensified, and the "chairman with seven souls" seemed to have played out his last trick.

It was against this gloomy atmosphere that the news on the initialing of an Israeli-Palestinian agreement in Oslo on August 20, 1993, struck like a thunderbolt. Soon an "inevitable" causality had been established, and all professional pessimists ran for cover. The declaration of principles and agreement on mutual recognition of the PLO and Israel were truly astonishing documents; almost too good to be true. The historic handshake between Yitzhak Rabin and Yassir Arafat on the lawn of the White House on September 13, 1993, was a supremely symbolic act, transforming the Israeli-Palestinian feud from a primordial shepherds' war into a rational, solvable conflict. It had redefined the enmity: Israelis and Palestinians had been transformed from demonic foes into legitimate enemies. Thus a precondition of any negotiation was met: recognition of the legitimacy, autonomy, and authority of the representatives of the other collective entity. Nothing had been resolved, but a marketplace had been established, and give-and-take procedures had been defined.

The import of that momentous event must be measured against the background of the basic, existential conflict that characterized the Israeli-Palestinian confrontation. A hundred years of violent conflict have left residues of fear, hatred, revenge, dehumanization, and brutalization of values. A century has produced dichotomous, tribal, militant worldviews, psychological fixations and irrational perceptions. On those foundations, saturated with blood and hatred, educational systems, destructive myths, despicable stereotypes, organs of coercive control, dual legal and administrative bodies, terrorism and counterterrorism were created and fostered. Violence growing out of the conflict created bureaucracies that viewed violence and confrontation as givens, and responded accordingly, thus exacerbating the conflict. Intimate enmity has made the two communities into mirror images, swaying in a dance of death, clutched in a fatal embrace. The Jewish community, stronger and more developed than its enemy, wished to overwhelm the Palestinian community and thus win peace and tranquility. But the Palestinian community, against all logic, refused to acknowledge defeat and continued the violent struggle, denying the Jews the fruits of their victory. Violence could not end the conflict; on the contrary, it stoked it in an endless cycle of murder and revenge.

To understand the Israeli and Palestinian heritage of hatred, one must return to the formative experiences that have shaped the consciousness of the two sides since the dawn of the tragic encounter between them. The hardship and danger of settling in a new and unfamiliar land, inhabited by a hostile indigenous people, has been imprinted on the Israeli consciousness. The Palestinians continued to relive the alien intrusion into their territory and the trauma of their dispossession, which has not ceased for 100 years and has made them fear for their very existence as a community. Educational, economic, military, social, and political institutions have all been constructed as adversarial systems designed to deal with those threats, but the most potent defense mechanism was the creation of elaborate myths.

Myths are the building-blocks from which a society constructs its collective self-image. The myth is the battle cry and the lullaby, the makeup and the gown, the screen and the lens used by human societies to rouse people to action, to live dreams, to blur ugly lines, to cope with an unpleasant reality, to find consolation and channel hatred, to curry favor with foreigners and foster a positive self-image. Myths are not illusions; they are a jumble of real and legendary events that have been stuck together with the glue of heroic and traumatic experiences, easily ingested; the minute they are absorbed, they become truer than reality itself. Many aspire to shatter myths, and so force people to confront objective truth. But the attempt to rip away this façade cannot succeed, because it amounts to an attack on the collective self-identity. It will, therefore, be met with anger. There is no need for this, because the myths a society adopts for itself are the best testimony to its sensitivities, weaknesses, dilemmas, and collective identity, its boldness in distorting reality and the image it wishes to present to the world and to itself.

Realization of the Zionist dream involved objective and subjective difficulties, which brought on distress and remorse; these in turn created powerful myths to cope with the given reality, and when the Zionist enterprise succeeded, they became absolute, eternal truths, good for all time. The change in objective circumstances did no harm to the credibility of the old myth; quite the opposite—success was irrefutable proof that it was true. Thus, when circumstances changed, myths originally created to bridge contradictory values, to mitigate ideological distress, to resolve inconsistencies between universalism and nationalism, between humanism and bloodshed, between equality and discrimination, turned into devices for self-justification and psychological evasions, instruments for the distortion of reality.

The shrines of Jewish Last Stands are the symbols of the security myth created by the Israeli-Arab conflict. There is Masada, the last stronghold of the Zealots of the Great Revolt, who chose to kill themselves rather than fall into the hands of their Roman enemies. There is Tel Hai, a settlement that fell to the Arabs, its revered commander crying, "It is good to die for one's country!" as he perished. "Masada shall not fall again"; "Conquer the hill or die"; "Few against many"; "Sheaves and swords"; "The purity of arms"; and "Self-restraint" were among the ideals these produced.

The security myth was nurtured by the leadership of the small, beleaguered Jewish community, which was forced to defend itself covertly and with meager means against Arab violence during the British Mandate, when neither it nor the Arabs had sovereign authority. This myth was bound up with the moral soul-searching of people with humanist sensibilities, people who were repelled by the use of force for its own sake. Political considerations and the lack of weapons on the one hand and moral values on the other united in a policy mandating that force be used for self-defense only, with minimum bloodshed. Decisive Jewish victories on the battlefield and the ongoing military confrontation have together fortified the element of force in Israeli identity at the expense of the humanist elements. This was intensified as Israel's military power grew and came to be seen as the sole means by which the conflict could be brought to an end. The battle cry of the few, the weak, and the desperate turned into the thunder of artillery and the clatter of engines in a huge army serving a sovereign state.

There is a tendency to blame the founding fathers for having ignored the "Arab question," to criticize them for having been ignorant, blind, naive, or arrogant when it came to understanding the real character of the conflict. Their humanist-socialist value system did not allow them to reach the inevitable conclusion that in order to realize Zionism's aims, even in its constructivist-socialist version, it was necessary to defeat the Arabs by force. The statement often quoted in this context is one made by David Ben-Gurion in 1924: "Zionism does not have a moral right to harm even one Arab child, even if at that price it may realize all its objectives."

Ignoring the character of the conflict amounts to self-delusion or sheer blindness. Yet the ideological contortions of Zionist thought and its conscious attempts to evade these dilemmas prove manifestly that the fundamental nature of the conflict and its dynamics were familiar to the founding fathers. Precisely because it was clear to them that there was no chance for compromise on the basis of Arab recognition of Zionist aspirations, they devoted great intellectual effort to fostering an ideology that would bridge unresolvable contradictions. Their political and social precepts, and their sensitivity to humanist values, forced them to take positions and nurture myths meant to make their Zionist aspirations compatible with their universalist values. This demonstrated the power of the myth as a means of uniting unre-solvable opposites, of interpreting a difficult reality, mitigating ideological distress, conveying consolation and hope, mobilizing public opinion, and molding the next generation in its own image. The convoluted ideological formulas seem, in the per-spective of years, to be naive, evasive, even hypocritical, but the myth that cloaked the ideology seemed credible and perennial. The years have not weathered it; on the contrary, they have cov-ered it with a protective patina. It has become a fundamental ele-ment in Israeli and Jewish identity.

The founding fathers were well aware of the charges against the Zionist enterprise and the negative image their enemies spread. They responded to criticism from without, and doubts from within, by creating a powerful myth that may be summa-rized as follows: An ancient nation, dispersed and persecuted, has risen up to realize the words of its prophets, to gather in its Dias-pora, to return to ruined Zion, to redeem its wilderness with manual labor, and to establish an egalitarian society, based on material and spiritual values that will once again make the Jewish people a light unto the nations. The Zionist enterprise is not a society of colonial settlers; it is a national liberation movement. It may have its source in the Jewish religion, but that is an ethnic religion containing solid national foundations. The Jews came to the Land of Israel not because they needed living space, but because they wished to return to their homeland, for which they had yearned for two thousand years. Unlike other white settlers, they settled in their land without the aid of a mother country. Like the other nations of the Third World, they fought for their independence, expelled the British imperialists, and established a sovereign state. They then had to defend their homeland against repeated attempts by the Arab countries to destroy it. The Zionists did not steal the land from its inhabitants; they redeemed a barren waste. The Hebrew pioneer did not fight people; he fought against forces of nature. He made the desert bloom and healed the wounds of ecological neglect—the felled forests, the overgrazed vegetation, the broken terraces, the blocked rivers, the malignant swamps.

No, ran this Zionist mythologizing, the land was not empty, but there is room enough for all. The Jews have no need to dispossess anyone, so long as they do not impede the realization of the Zionist dream. The Arab residents of the land are an inseparable part of the Arab nation, which has more than twenty sovereign states. The Arabs of Palestine do not constitute a national group, and in any case many of them are recent arrivals, attracted by jobs created by Jewish economic development. The Jews did not establish a separate society and separatist institutions, employ Hebrew labor, and create separate education and housing projects because they were racist and wanted to distance the Arabs and discriminate against them. In fact, they specifically wanted to avoid creating a colonial society based on an upper, European class ruling over exploited peons. The hostility of the Arabs will disappear eventually, as they come to recognize the value of the progress that the Jews brought them; most Arabs wish for peace, but were incited by landed notables disguised as national leaders. Arab violence is not an expression of a legitimate aspiration to national liberation; it is instead cruel terror aimed at destroying the Zionist enterprise. The hostility of the Palestinians is absolute and irrational; during World War II, they supported the Nazis, and in 1947, when the Jews agreed to a painful compromise—the partition of the land—the Palestinians refused because they did not accept, and will never accept, the existence of a Jewish state anywhere in the Land of Israel.

This, then, was the burden Yitzhak Rabin carried on his shoulders when he turned and faced PLO leader Yassir Arafat on the green lawn of the White House. And what heritage had Arafat brought with him? He and his people had no need to create elaborate myths designed to justify the destruction of another people so that theirs would thrive, and neither did he feel compelled to reconcile dispossession with liberal-socialist values. He carried with him the raw feelings of anguish, rage, and despair shared by millions who had been forced to flee their homes and orchards. Dispersed to the four corners of the earth, living in the squalor of refugee camps, rejected by their own Arab brethren, they have literally kept the keys to their homes, long destroyed and covered by Israel's highways and industrial plants. "The only reason for their existence is the thought that soon they will find their house once again, with the color of its stones, the smell of its gardens, the water of its fountains, all intact, unaltered, just as it has been in their dreams." This is how Amin Ma'alouf has described their emotions, using the metaphor of the longing for al-Andalus—the lost paradise of Muslim Spain. Their sense of loss was intensified by a sense of the injustice of their having had to pay for the wickedness of others who had persecuted the Jews, forcing them to flee and displace them. The impotent rage instilled into them by repeated defeats coalesced around a simple yet potent concept: "al-'Auda"—The Return. It is a challenge to reality, a firm belief that defeat is the herald of the inevitable victory, that the glorious past will come back, that there are no losses that are not regained and no fatal calamity—provided one does not give up belief in a just cause. "The Return" does not necessarily mean actual repossession of the houses, gardens, and fountains of a past era, but rather the in-gathering of Palestinian exiles and the reconstruction of Palestine "from the river to the sea."

When Arafat extended his hands to Yitzhak Rabin, he acted in the realm of reality. By shaking the hand of the first and only native prime minister of Israel, a scion of the Zionist founding fathers, he committed an act of surrender. Out of responsibility to his vanquished people, he asked for terms and begged for the magnanimity of the victors. For he reckoned that there was no other option but to admit defeat.

If it is painfully hard to admit defeat, it is not easy to believe in victory. Indeed, many observers, including this writer, could not believe that the Palestinians' hope that reality was transient—and Israelis' fears that their enemies were right—would ever permit them to shake hands.

A few months before the historic handshake, I borrowed Albert Camus's description of the French-Algerian conflict to characterize the Israeli-Palestinian conflict: "It is as if two insane people, crazed with wrath, had decided to turn into a fatal embrace, a forced marriage from which they cannot free themselves. Forced to live together and incapable of uniting, they decided at last to die together." I defined the conflict as intercommunal: an ongoing confrontation between two human collectives, struggling for natural and human resources, and competing for exclusive control over symbolic assets within a territorial unit that both consider their homeland. It is a multifaceted and multilayered conflict. On the one hand, it is a political, national-ethnic struggle for sovereignty. On the other hand, it is typical of divided societies and derives from an unequal division of resources, asymmetrical economic dependency, and a monopoly over state coercive power exercised by one group against the other. Intercommunal conflicts are organic and endemic, a never-ending twilight war. At best, violence sinks beneath the surface, but the potential for a conflagration is ever present.

The distinction between internal, communal conflict and external, interstate conflict is fundamental. An interstate dispute is conducted in a defined international framework made up of sovereign states. These sovereign entities are legitimate actors and treat one another as equals. Sovereign states reach decisions based on concrete, pragmatic considerations, in which ideology plays a secondary role. Conflicts of interest between states may be defined and formulated, and the process of solving them has been developed and polished over centuries of diplomatic activity. Diplomatic conflict resolution rests on the perception that the participants are fully accredited, and that no participant has authority over any other. Each participant represents an independent regime responsible to specific and recognized national groups. The subject of the negotiations is not the fundamental status of each side as a separate and autonomous entity, but rather the conditions and circumstances under which the autonomous entities act, and how they manage the legitimate conflicts of interest between them.

The intercommunal conflict revolves around fundamental questions of identity, disputes over symbolic assets (a homeland, symbols of sovereignty), and absolute justice. An intercommunal conflict is perceived as a struggle over the supreme value—collective survival—on which there can be no compromise. The two sides may talk in rational, pragmatic language in their diplomatic contacts. But these are only rhetorical devices that conceal a hidden agenda of absolute values. The attempt to apply the interstate conceptual world fails because a precondition of any negotiation is recognition of the legitimacy, autonomy, and authority of the representatives of the other collective—yet nonrecognition of all these is, indeed, the very heart of the intercommunal conflict.

The chances that a real change would occur, I concluded, were not great. Even though the Israeli-Palestinian conflict has already lasted for a hundred years, it is still not ripe for a solution. Were the Palestinians able to overcome their shame-honor complex and their dreams of messianic salvation, for which current reality is merely preparation, they would acknowledge their defeat and adopt a more pragmatic strategy. Were the Israelis to perceive reality as it is, rather than as what it is distorted into by the prism of their myths, they would understand that they have won and must therefore abandon their traditional paranoia and come to terms with the legitimacy of the Palestinian collective and its material and symbolic needs.

Were both sides at least to understand the simple fact that the two communities are doomed to live side by side forever, and that neither can destroy the other, the conflict would be ripe for a solution. In the meantime, and in the foreseeable future, the existing geopolitical conditions would prevail. Israel, being in possession of an overwhelming military and economic power, would continue to rule the entire territory between the Jordan and the sea, whether directly or through autonomous Palestinian institutions with limited powers. It would be a dynamic, violent, and volatile geopolitical status quo, but it would remain confined to western Palestine and to the peoples sharing that land. The interstate conflict with neighboring Arab countries would be resolved. This pessimistic prognosis earned its notoriety as the "irreversibility thesis."

The unfolding events and especially the signing of the declaration of Israeli-Palestinian mutual recognition have stunned me. With the touch of a wand, my pessimistic determinism crumbled before my eyes. The declaration reads: "[The two sides] agree that it is time to put an end to decades of confrontation and conflict, recognize their mutual legitimate and political rights, and strive to live in peaceful coexistence and mutual dignity and security." This almost routine sentence put an end to a bloody ideological strife, at least on the formal, diplomatic plane. It created the "ripening point," which I had identified but could not believe the parties were able to achieve.

When asking myself where I erred, I detected one basic fault: my own romantic perception of the Israeli-Palestinian conflict gave excessive weight to its ideological and emotional elements. Infused with anachronisms and nostalgia myself, I gravitated to and identified with the tragedy, failing to perceive how drawn people are to catharsis. I did not assign the proper weight to historical processes and overlooked the political demands and objective constraints on leaders, who must react to the needs and attitudes of their constituencies and see themselves as historical actors.

The emotional-ideological disposition that influenced my thinking can easily be discerned: I belong to the minority of Israelis who still view the conflict through an ideological prism. My late father, one of Israel's founding fathers, inculcated me with a profound attachment to Zionist ideology. Foremost in my education has been a great love, tangible and spiritual, for the land of my birth, extending over the dimensions of both time and space, and strong identification with the pioneering ethos. I was well aware of how that secular religion has been perverted into a messianic fundamentalist pornography, how the old myths have been manipulated to serve as an excuse for plunder and injustice. I abhorred and condemned the Israeli right-wing political culture, and especially "Gush Emunim" settlers, who tried to expropriate the halo of the founding fathers, a halo they had no part in earning, in order to surround their deeds with the pioneering myths' aura of respectability.

At the same time, I could not identify with the opposite political culture, that of "Peace Now," which sought to free itself from the burden of the old myths and in the process discarded the basic value of love for the homeland. From their safe haven in hedonistic Tel Aviv, which the founding fathers toiled to build and defend, they tarnished the pioneering ethos in a direct retort to attempts by the right to manipulate it. The left believed that they were pursuing a rational policy, divorced from the old myths tying Israelis to bygone quarrels. But in fact, they created a romantic, emotional, ideal notion of peace, and in doing so, they were as irrational as their right-wing opponents.

I could not join in the jubilation at the prospect of "getting rid of the territories." I was ready to cede parts of the homeland in the context of a rational process of negotiations, but felt that such an act amounted to a painful tearing of raw flesh. I mourned the perversion of the old values as much as I regretted their waning, and believed that it was possible to adapt them to changed circumstances.

Busy fending off attacks from both right and left, I failed to realize that the entire ideological debate, including my own contribution, had become anachronistic. The Israeli public was bored with the old shibboleths and perceived the Israeli-Palestinian conflict in pragmatic terms: they wished to get rid of the Arabs and felt that the burden of controlling a hostile and murderous population interfered with their main concern: pursuing the ideals of the consumer society. A desire for "separation" prompted by hatred, boredom, alienation, and weariness of violence—not ideological commitment to peace—was the source of the public support that enabled Yitzhak Rabin to sign the declaration that stunned, infuriated, and cheered the likes of me.

My ideological, romantic, and emotional disposition equally influenced my perceptions of Palestinian stances and attitudes. Precisely because of my own native sense of belonging to the homeland, I understood their passion and respected their emotion. A shared sentiment prevails between us—it is the sentiment that makes us all both children of the same land and blood enemies. The outline of our native land's panorama that my father etched on my consciousness is composed not only of the physical landscape, flora, and fauna, but of people, and it follows that there is no Eretz Israel without Arabs. The Hebrew map on one level of my consciousness is intertwined with a second, Arab level. I am well aware of the great bond to their birthplaces that millions of Palestinians keep secure in their hearts.

The painful memories of Palestine lost, the remorse and rage, the longing and despair would not allow them, I thought, to give up the dreams of The Return. I admit that it did not occur to me that the Palestinians could reach such a state of weakness and go through a period of such desperation that they would recognize defeat and allow those who had brought catastrophe upon them to dictate the conditions of their surrender. Indeed, had I been a

Palestinian, I would have been among those—mainly intellectuals, writers, and poets—from Edward Said to Mahmoud Darwish, who rejected and opposed the Israeli-Palestinian agreements. As an Israeli, I felt that one might nod one's head and reflect upon the judgment of history, but a world separated me from those who purported to be sensitive to the plight of others—and shouted with joy.

The triumph of reason over emotion was truly magnificent, but questions lingered. Is this merely a peace between political elites that leaves the masses still permeated with the old irrational disposition? Does the Temple Mount massacre of October 8, 1990, represent the true nature of the conflict—and was the ceremony on the lawn of the White House merely an episode? Has the breakthrough created the energy and commitment essential to transforming the lives of ordinary people, thus making peace a concrete, meaningful condition. Does the new phase, in which the demonic foe has become a legitimate enemy, lead inevitably to compromise or merely sharpen the dilemma over whether to make peace or do battle?

I had definitely erred in defining the "ripening point" of the conflict, but did I err in diagnosing it as an organic intercommunal conflict confined to Israel/Palestine? Have the agreements in fact changed the character of the human and collective interaction between the two communities, or have they merely redefined the dispute and established new rules of engagement?

The declaration of principles, negotiations leading to the agreement on self-rule in the occupied territories, and subsequent developments seem to attest to the validity of the intercommunal theory, supporting the conclusion that the Israeli-Palestinian conflict has shrunk to its original core, both in space and in essence. Unfolding events—negotiations, agreements, violence, attitudes, rhetoric, economic developments—have manifested the unaltered nature of the conflict: an organic struggle between two collectives over the physical, material, and symbolic resources of a shared homeland. The interstate conflict between Israel and the neighboring Arab countries has lost its ideological context and turned into a relatively simple international dispute, and it has thus gone a long way toward resolution.

There is no better person to attest to the validity of the intercommunal thesis than Yassir Arafat himself. By signing the Oslo documents, he has gone so far as to cast the lot of the Palestinian people with Israel. He turned his back on his Arab brothers, gave up the dream of liberating Palestine by the charge of Arab cavalry and Arab petrodollars, or through the machinations of the Russian empire. Harsh reality forced him to seek shelter under the aegis of his mortal enemy, nourishing the hope that he would be able to effect change from within. Bitter experience showed him the unreliability of both the Arab states' ideological commitment to the Palestinian cause and their actual support. This is not merely because of their weakness or selfishness. No country in the world can act solely based on the dictates of ethnic solidarity. The complexity of the interstate system forces sovereign states to balance their own interests against their ethnic loyalties. When Greece understood in 1974 that its interests required it to improve its relations with Turkey, it abandoned the Greek Cypriots. Similarly, the Indian government trod carefully in Sri Lanka, where its ethnic links with the Tamil minority forced it into active involvement in the civil war with the Sinhalese but self-interest later led it to withdraw. The Dublin government takes care not to involve itself in the civil war in Northern Ireland and gives no support to the radical Catholics, even though their goal is to unite with the Irish Republic.

The Arab countries have always swayed between absolute support for the Palestinians (including the planning and execution of terrorist acts against Israel), and apathy, even hostility. Their position has been determined by their own needs and only marginally by the requirements of ethnic solidarity. When it was in their interest to make agreements with Israel, they did so, while hiding behind the fig leaf of pro-Palestinian rhetoric. When the cease-fire agreements of 1949 were signed, the Palestinians screamed that they were "a second Balfour Declaration"; the Camp David accords and the peace treaty between Egypt and Israel were considered "a knife in the back of the Palestinian people."

The Arab "brother states" watched in silence when the Israelis destroyed Arafat's quasi-independent center in Beirut, and they saw to it that his new asylum would be at arm's length from Israel, in Tunis. The end of Pan-Arab nationalism, so clearly manifested by the Gulf War, dealt a final blow to the Palestinian cause as a potent rallying cry. The "president of the State of Palestine" had never been weaker and more isolated than when his enemy Yitzhak Rabin threw him a life preserver.

Rabin did not act out of compassion or empathy: in fact, he despised and mistrusted Arafat. He needed him as a partner in managing the raging intercommunal strife, however, and also to serve as a witness that his promise of peace in six or nine months had not been an empty boast. Rabin calculated that Arafat's demise would usher in Hamas and that by saving Arafat he was taking only a small risk. He could rely on his superior might, and assured the Israelis that he was acting "from a position of power."

He knew that by moving to the territories, Arafat would become even more dependent on the Israelis than he had ever been on the countries of his exile—Jordan, Lebanon, and even Tunisia. The vast power disparity between Israel and the PLO is evident in the Oslo documents and has been even more salient during the implementation process. It is no accident that during all the meetings held between Arafat and Rabin, the former declared resignedly: "You hold the power" or "You have the upper hand."

The declaration of principles has gone a long way toward realizing Palestinian aspirations. In it Israel recognizes their right "to govern themselves" as a people, thus implying that they have the right of self-determination. The first phase, withdrawal from Gaza and Jericho, created an irreversible step toward their exercising self-determination, for Israel's control over those areas, according to international law, was based on effective military control, and once relinquished, cannot be reimposed. Therefore, even if an agreement on the final disposition of the territories is not achieved, the Palestinian authority's territorial control would fulfill the basic conditions for recognition as a state. The West Bank and Gaza have been recognized as "a single territorial unit, whose integrity will be preserved during the interim period."

The Green Line has thus been reestablished. The elected council of the self-governing authority has been granted legislative, executive, and extensive economic powers, judicial organs, and control of the physical infrastructure of the territories. The picture of a state in an advanced stage of formation is completed by a strong police force—civilian police, militia, and secret services—and other symbols of statehood, such as stamps, identity cards, and travel documents. Yassir Arafat could thus present his people with great achievements, which, he believed, enabled

May 1994, after protracted and sometimes strained negotiations. The lengthy documents, containing hundreds of clauses, provisions, and annexes, prompted one outspoken Israeli cabinet minister to say: "Had the British imposed so many restrictions, the State of Israel would not have been established." This was an understatement, for in this case the "British" (to use the same metaphor) never left the "liberated territories." Moreover, the Palestinians had legitimized the continued presence of the occupier. Gaza and Jericho under Palestinian authority resembled a protectorate of "Palestan" more than they did a State of Palestine.

Israeli forces withdrew from these areas, and a Palestinian authority with legislative and executive powers took over. But the withdrawal was far from complete, and the powers granted to the Palestinian authority have thus far been partial. The Israeli forces were "redeployed" in the Katif settlement block, which remains under exclusive Israeli jurisdiction. Israeli forces can freely use the roads within Gaza and Jericho, and access roads to Israeli settlements, which crisscross the Gaza Strip, remain under exclusive Israeli control. Even after withdrawal, the Israeli Military Government retains its powers "in accordance with international law," and the Palestinian authority can change the existing laws and military orders only "if it does not threaten Israeli interests." Under no circumstances will the Palestinian authority have any jurisdiction over Israelis (individuals, agencies, or corporations). Israel ceases to bear any financial responsibility for Gaza and Jericho, and any financial claims against Israel for acts prior to the transfer of authority are to be referred to the Palestinians. In short, all Israeli interests have been secured and a precedent established that, if applied to the rest of the occupied territories, would amount to a diktat, or, to put it differently—the occupation continues, albeit by remote control, and with the consent of the Palestinian people, represented by their "sole representative," the PLO.

The economic agreements reinforce the impression of total capitulation. Under the thin veil of respectability provided by terms such as "common market," "customs envelope," "integrated Israeli-Palestinian economy," and "equal status," the preexisting economic relations remain almost unaltered. The Palestinians remain dependent on Israel in all spheres of economic activity. Provisions such as that providing for "free movement of workers, subject to the right of each side to determine the size and conditions of movement of workers to its area" serve as an example of the false symmetry: as if there were a single Israeli worker eager to find employment in Gaza, compared to the tens of thousands of Gazans who cannot survive without employment in Israel. The quasi-colonial economic relationship persists, as shown by the following statistics: two million Palestinians, one-third of the population of western Palestine (Israel and the territories) control only 8 percent of its water resources and 13 percent of the land; they generate 5 percent of Israel's gross domestic product; their industrial production is equivalent to that of a single medium-sized Israeli plant; and their per capita income is one-tenth that of Israelis.

A World Bank report describes the conditions in the occupied territories as "imbalanced and distorted": "heavy dependence on outside sources, an unusually low degree of industrialization, a trade structure heavily dominated by trading links with Israel and with a large trade deficit and inadequacies in the provision of public infrastructure and services." The economy has been heavily dependent on employment in Israel, which accounted for almost a third of the territories' gross domestic product. The trade deficit with Israel amounted to 28 percent of their gross national product in the 1980s. Agriculture production was stagnating or shrinking because of severe restrictions on irrigation and limits on agricultural exports to Israel, while the territories were kept wide open to the marketing of Israeli produce. Manufacturing was predominantly based on small cottage industries. The average per capita urban supply of water was half that in Jordan, and electricity consumption per capita was two-thirds of that in Egypt. One-third of Palestinian villages had no centrally supplied electricity and only eighty out of four hundred villages had telephone service. Public expenditures on health, education, and welfare were extremely low, resulting in substandard education and poor health facilities. The total budget of the Israeli occupation's administration equaled that of a medium-sized Israeli town.

Harsh criticism of the Israeli policies and practices responsible for these deplorable conditions was not new. Researchers and political opponents have long exposed Israel's policies and their consequences, given the lie to the myth of a "benign occupation," and refuted the legend of the economic and social progress made during a generation of Israeli rule. The novelty has been that the same persons and authorities who shared responsibility for the disastrous situation—and who had vehemently rejected all criticism of it, sometimes even labeling critics as traitors—suddenly began to circulate such reports. They were now keen to exploit the misery of the Palestinians as a tool for mobilizing international compassion and collecting funds for them. The grim conditions in the territories, it seems, had suddenly arisen out of thin air. There were no Israeli expressions of remorse or admissions of guilt, merely pronouncements about "economic development as a basis for political compromise" and "the necessity to make peace palatable through improvement of living conditions."

The initiators of the Oslo process firmly believed in the semi-colonialist, semi-Marxist theory that peace and reconciliation depend on improvement of living conditions and economic prosperity. As a result, the declaration of principles devotes disproportionate space to questions of economics and development. In recognition of the "mutual benefit" to be derived from cooperating in developing the occupied territories, an Israeli-Palestinian Economic Cooperation Committee has been established to supervise development plans dealing with social reconstruction, housing and construction, small businesses, infrastructure (water, electricity, communications, and transportation), human resources, and other areas—in fact, all the areas so badly neglected by Israel.

One may wonder why the "link between peace and prosperity" was discovered only after Israel relinquished its responsibilities. The parties jointly solicited funds from "donor states" and got generous commitments. Israel flatly refused to allocate "a single penny," in the words of its finance minister. Indeed, the Gaza and Jericho agreement provides that all Israel's financial responsibilities, including that for acts prior to the transfer of authority, are to be borne by the Palestinians. One may wonder why the Palestinians allowed the Israelis to wipe the slate clean, when it was a known fact that Israel had collected huge sums in a "deduction fund"—money withheld from the earnings of Palestinian workers for social security benefits (to equalize the cost of their employment with that of Israeli workers, so that Palestinians would not have the advantage of being cheaper) and kept in Israel's treasury.

The Israelis discovered soon enough that Chairman Arafat had his own interpretation of the link between finance and politics. He insisted that all contributions from donors be channeled through him, refused to establish a "transparent" distribution system, and controlled expenditures on development projects. When donors refused to give the chairman "walking-around money," and the desperately needed financial aid failed to arrive, the Israelis took it upon themselves to "expedite the process." After all, they sought stability, and it was in their interest to strengthen Arafat, even when it meant that orderly financing would not be in accordance with "Western standards." Other embarrassing violations of accepted norms also emerged: Chairman Arafat closed down opposition newspapers, and Palestinian police tortured prisoners. The Israeli director of the Civil Rights Association stated: "Outside Israeli jurisdiction, there is no place for the association's involvement."

The declaration of principles provided for the establishment of a permanent committee to supervise cooperation in a long list of areas, such as water, electricity and energy, finance and international investment and banking, the port of Gaza, communication and transport, industry, labor relations, human resources, and protection of the environment. The long list of areas in which cooperation and coordination is essential points to one basic fact that the advocates of "separation" have yet to grasp: the country, from the Jordan to the sea, can perhaps be divided politically, but not physically.

Israelis and Palestinians share a considerable part of their water resources, and they must therefore cooperate in the utilization and management of water resources (including control of sewage and overpumping). Cooperation is also essential in almost every other aspect of human activity, from air pollution to waste disposal; from physical planning to access to beaches and holy places. Israel had monopolized natural resources and harnessed the environment to satisfy its interests. The constant references to "cooperation in the West Bank and Gaza" indicate that while Israel is free to act independently in its own sovereign area, it insists on "coordinating" the usage of natural resources by the Palestinians, so that Israeli interests will not be harmed. This asymmetry perpetuates the existing inequality in the distribution of common natural resources and reemphasizes the impression of a victor's peace. For the Israelis, it is a peace without pain or sacrifice; a bargain proposition, compatible with the atmosphere of a de-ideologized consumer society. Pragmatic, even selfish attitudes can serve as powerful incentives for supporting peace. However, such attitudes depend on instant gratification and have as their corollary unwillingness to bear the short-term costs of long-term benefits. Israelis enjoyed the short-term benefits of separation and the ceremonies of peace. But only painful compromises over real assets that they consider their own can bring about peace, for the inequality is so vast, and the Palestinians will not suffer it for long. Israeli leaders enjoyed public support for their bold decisions, but they failed to prepare their public for the inevitable need to invest real assets to achieve a durable peace.

Material assets are expandable, anonymous, and commonplace; symbolic assets are fixed, unique, and dear. The Israelis had to bear a heavy price in symbolic terms, if one compares their myths with the symbolic actions taken by their leaders. First they had to change their perception of the archenemy, the PLO, responsible for murdering women and children, and then to accept it as a partner in negotiations on giving up parts of their homeland. Secondly, they had to contend with the symbols of a Palestinian collective entity—flags, uniforms, delegations—that collided with their perception of themselves as the sole legitimate community in their country. Then came the ultimate test—the return of Yassir Arafat.

The homecoming of the exiled leader, after almost fifty years of wandering, had been perceived by many as a supremely symbolic event. Many Palestinians viewed it as a sign heralding the beginning of "The Return," a decisive step on the road leading to the liberation of Jerusalem. Israeli right-wing politicians tried to raise a public protest and organized demonstrations with the slogan "Arafat the murderer will not pass." Foreign television networks brought in large crews to report on Arafat's triumphal entry.

Yet the return was a non-event. The Palestinians were too harassed by the hardships of daily life to experience elation and express emotion. After all, the peace process and the withdrawal from Gaza and Jericho have not changed their conditions, and even made them worse. Unemployment in Gaza increased, prices doubled, and thousands of Palestinians remained in Israeli detention camps. Opposition to the peace process mounted and Hamas openly challenged Arafat's authority. The Palestinian authority and the militant Islamic forces moved on an inevitable collision course. When the clash occurred and Palestinians shot Palestinians, a blood account was opened, and once opened could not easily be closed.

On the West Bank, bureaucratic harassment by the military

government continued, as well as harsh reprisals for any act of violence, as if nothing had changed. Clashes with militant settlers were frequent, culminating in a terrible massacre of Muslim worshipers in the Tombs of the Patriarchs in Hebron, perpetrated by a settler from Kiryat Arba. Hamas militants began a new wave of suicide bombings to avenge the massacre of "Haram Ibrahimi," precisely like the wave of killings that followed the massacre on the Temple Mount. The Israeli authorities held the Palestinian authority responsible for the killings. When the harassed Palestinians made feeble attempts to apprehend the terrorists, they were labeled Israel's henchmen, and tension inside the Palestinian camp mounted. The pattern was too familiar, and people asked themselves, where is the peace?

Israelis should ostensibly have felt threatened by the return of the "hairy demon," the hated "two-legged beast," but most remained indifferent. After two days of prime-time coverage, Arafat's whereabouts barely merited a short item in the media. "Separation"—physical and psychological—from "the Arabs" turned Arafat's return into an internal Palestinian affair. He returned, not to Israel/Palestine, but to the "Autonomy," an isolated, distant island, where strange voodoo ceremonies are conducted in an incomprehensible language. Even the half-hearted protests subsided, and Likud leaders began to realize that it was their last chance. In future, they would not be able to exploit the irrational drives evoked by Arafat's personality. The Palestinian leader has lost his satanic aura, and his human, somewhat grotesque, features emerged.

Arafat drinking Israeli water, reading by light supplied by the Israel Electrical Corporation, and sending faxes through Israeli telephone lines is a domesticated Arafat. Beside the shining symbol of "The Return" walked its shadow—submission to Israel's overwhelming might and reliance on its magnanimity and willingness to assist, directly or indirectly, in the process of Palestinian nation-building. In his public statements, Arafat expressed the symbol and its shadow. After directing a chorus of thousands chanting, "With blood, with spirit we shall deliver you, O Filastin," he moved on to ask politely for Israeli assistance and permission to release prisoners. At times, he sounded like the leader of the latest Israeli pressure group, demanding, like the others—Israeli Arabs, Orthodox Jews, farmers, importers—that Yitzhak Rabin "do something for us." At times, it looked as though the days of the Mandate had returned, with one difference: the place of the British high commissioner had been taken by the prime minister of Israel.

Yitzhak Rabin has been aware of the danger in Arafat's developing dependence: Israel would become responsible for the Palestinians' economic malaise and would be called upon to render material assistance. Rabin has no wish to become Arafat's nanny, and his generosity in reallocating resources to rectify the inequality between the Israeli and Palestinian communities has been very limited. All Israelis have been relieved by the withdrawal from Gaza; some have considered it an enlightened and moral act. Only few have felt that it is no more than an escape from confronting the heavy burden of Israel's victory—a victory that uprooted the Palestinians from their homes and flung them on that strip of hardship and desperation that is Gaza. For twenty-six years, they could have attempted to heal the wounds in order to implant the roots of coexistence, equality, and mutual respect, but did nothing. In withdrawing, they have left Gaza to become Arafat's problem, and a heavy burden has been lifted from their consciences.

Yitzhak Rabin wanted to emulate De Gaulle, but Israel is not France, an imperial power withdrawing across the sea to its metropolitan territory, leaving the colony in the hands of revolutionaries and partisans-turned-bureaucrats. The Israelis merely evacuated a tiny province surrounded by and dependent on sovereign Israeli territory. They could not behave according to the colonial model and wash their hands of the colony and the fate of its inhabitants.

In most liberated territories, the new and inexperienced regimes collapsed, physical infrastructure was neglected, economic chaos prevailed, and civil wars raged. Citizens achieved their national aspirations but paid a heavy price in terms of personal security and economic development. Israel could not afford that scenario, because unrest, economic chaos, and bad management in the liberated territories are bound to spill over and affect the security and even the quality of life in its own territory. As much as the Israelis wished to turn their backs on Arafat's Gaza and Jericho, they could not disentangle themselves: as much as they wished to apply an extraneous interstate solution to an intercommunal conflict, it became apparent that mutual interdependence prevents a surgical solution. And Gaza has been the easiest part, for when negotiations focused on the West Bank, the problems mounted up: settlements and settlers, security, water, land, ecology, enforcement; and the Jerusalem enigma loomed on the horizon. Increasingly, it seems that the De Gaulle–Ben Bella model does not fit Rabin and Arafat; another couple are more comparable: South Africa's F. W. de Klerk and Nelson Mandela.

The Oslo process has been a heroic attempt to impose an interstate solution and suppress the intercommunal realities. Israel relied on its power to effect separation, but it remained doubtful whether the Palestinians would agree to bear alone the consequences of the "separate and unequal" arrangement that Arafat had agreed to accept. It is doubtful whether he took the risk after serious deliberation. If he did, then he also was aware that his separate deal with Israel would put the latter in a strategic position it eagerly sought: conducting bilateral negotiations with each Arab state separately; taking advantage of inter-Arab rivalry; exploiting Israel's close relations with the United States. Once the taboo on separate deals and insistence on "a comprehensive peace," designed by the Arab states to protect the Palestinians, were abrogated by the latter, the last ideological barrier had been lifted.

Yassir Arafat was dismayed and angry when he heard the dramatic announcement that peace between Israel and Jordan was pending, and that King Hussein and Yitzhak Rabin were to sign a declaration in Washington terminating the state of belligerency between their countries. The PLO chairman pretended that he had not understood the gamble he had taken in Oslo and in Cairo, not merely by reaching an agreement behind Hussein's back, but also by signing agreements that directly harm basic Jordanian interests. He counted on Hussein's passivity and vacillations and believed that revolutionary changes in the occupied territories that threaten to destroy the Jordanian economy and to upset the uneasy coexistence between Palestinians and Transjordanians would not prompt the king to take action. But the king surprised him and brought his cordial relations with Israeli leaders, long kept on a quasi-confidential level, into the open.

The Israelis were elated. How refreshing it was to deal with a real king and a real state. Israeli observers and participants in meetings with the Jordanians returned singing their praises: How efficient their army was, how dignified their king was, how rational and serious the talks had been. Comparison with the Palestinians lies behind all these impressions: the confused delegates, the poor preparatory work, the chaos, the disheveled policemen, the manipulative chairman. But besides the external impressions, there was a greater fascination: interstate negotiations are rational; conflict of interests is quantifiable; demarcation of boundaries, military matters, division of water resources, and economic issues can be discussed with a minimum of emotional input. Their outcome affects ordinary people only indirectly. Intercommunal negotiations are messy, involve countless details, and are often irrational and emotional. Their outcome directly affects every member of both communities. No wonder Israelis preferred the Jordanians to the Palestinians, and soon the old "Jordanian option" crept from the graveyard of illusions: perhaps it was not too late to reanimate it, thus resolving the "Palestinian question"?

But it was too late. The Hashemite king had disassociated himself from the West Bank in 1988 and had no wish (or power) to control the rebellious Palestinians. If eventually they become disgusted with Arafat's chaotic regime and turn to him, he will consider. In the meantime, he maintained his considerable influence on the West Bank through his supporters, mainly wealthy merchants and the religious establishment. Imbued with the tragic history of his family, who had lost the guardianship of the two holy cities of Arabia, and his personal loss of Jerusalem, Islam's third city in rank of holiness, he demanded from the

Israelis that they safeguard his "historic role" in Jerusalem. The Israelis were delighted to oblige: it helped them to distinguish between the religious aspect of Jerusalem, on which they are flexible, and the sovereignty issue, on which they are not. In addition, they knew that by granting Hussein's wish, they would inflame Palestinian-Jordanian rivalry, which indeed occurred. Arafat retaliated by harassing pro-Jordanian Palestinians and closing down newspapers financed by Jordan. But he could not do much to break the nutcracker he himself had assisted in forging, consisting of an Israeli arm and a Jordanian arm, in whose grip he now found himself.

King Hussein made a tactical error by agreeing to participate in, and even host, the peace ceremonies, for the legitimation-hungry Israelis got what they wanted but refused to pay the bill. When the Jordanians presented their concrete demands—the return of patches of desert and quantities of water allocated to them by old agreements—the Israelis feigned surprise: "If the Jordanians are going to be stubborn about water and territory, the haggling will go on for years!" Perhaps they can once again succeed in getting peace free of charge, especially since they have already dined at the king's table. After all, the American president, who badly needed the peace ceremonies, had already paid generously, and the U.S. secretary of state had become expert at cutting ribbons at Israeli-Jordanian border crossings. It was only in the wake of a serious escalation of Hamas terrorism, causing universal outrage and a dramatic drop in public support, that Yitzhak Rabin cut through the red tape and concluded the negotiations with Jordan in one day. Peace ceremonies resumed with a vengeance, and the Israeli jet set vied for invitations to state banquets and cocktail parties.

The peace ceremonies, and even the successful negotiations on bilateral issues with Jordan were merely a pleasant break from the real intercommunal problems, in which Jordan is directly involved. The Israeli-Palestinian-Jordanian triangle could not easily be broken. West Bankers were still Jordanian subjects, the Jordanian dinar was legal tender on the West Bank, hundreds of thousands of Palestinian refugees crowded Jordanian cities, and the Palestinians expelled from Arabia after the Gulf War brought the Hashemite kingdom to the verge of bankruptcy. The Jordanians demanded that 800,000 Palestinians be allowed to return to their homeland, and Israel refused. The Paris and Cairo economic agreements kept the Palestinian economy within the Israeli envelope, erecting an economic wall between western Palestine and the outside world. The Jordanian economy paid the price: West Bankers exchanged their dinars in massive quantities, which flooded the Jordanian Central Bank; Israeli customs duties prevented Jordanian exports; Jordanians were cut off from channeling foreign aid to the Palestinians. Arafat was well aware of the damage caused to Jordan, but his advisers assured him that the Palestinians would be better off attached to the flourishing Israeli economy than to bankrupt Jordan. Anyway, the Israelis would not have it otherwise, for the alternative—creating economic borders between Israel and the territories—is contrary to their interests. There was a lengthy and complicated agenda on the tripartite table, but the core problem remained firmly rooted in the intercommunal interaction, and the real dialogue evolved around the management of the internal conflict.

The achievements of the Oslo process have been spectacular because both sides agreed to gradualism. Once they had crossed the threshold of mutual recognition, they assumed that both

with the binational reality and the radical demographic and physical changes that have occurred since 1967. Seven million people now live in the territory between the Jordan and the Mediterranean. The interrelations that have developed and the utilization of natural and human resources have created a situation that can no longer be dealt with by completely cutting off and separating the communities from each other. This mutual dependence is expressed in the areas of economics, employment, demography, security, waste disposal, water and land management, physical planning, ecology, transportation, taxes, law, and administration—and in all other spheres of human activity. Indeed, all the documents of the Oslo process address the need for close cooperation. Those who support a geographical and political separation into two national states, Israeli and Palestinian, also recognize this mutual dependence. All plans for a permanent solution emphasize the need for joint coordination and oversight mechanisms to regulate intercommunal relations. The areas in which such coordination is necessary for the benefit of all are so broad, and the areas that can be placed under the sole control of either side are so small, that even the advocates of geopolitical separation envision a political system that resembles a confederation.

It goes without saying that "cooperation" based on the current power relationship is no more than permanent Israeli domination in disguise, and that Palestinian self-rule is merely a euphemism for bantustanization. Permanent geopolitical separation is viewed as a remedy, for it creates political equality, on the basis of which genuine cooperation between sovereign states can be achieved. Yet the Palestinians would surely strive to realize the ideals embodied in the concepts of "sovereignty," "independence," and "self-determination" in full, and therefore attempt to achieve autarchy, or—at least—freedom from an enforced bond with their overwhelmingly stronger partner. The Israelis, whose vital interests would be affected by such unilateral actions, would react harshly. The interplay between separation and coordination, independent action and the real power relationships, are amply manifested in the Oslo process and clearly documented in the written agreements.

It is obvious that the simplistic slogan "Two states for two peoples" requires very intricate interpretation—indeed, innovative political thinking. The need to combine political separation with physical unity, separate national self-identity with strong affinity to the shared homeland, points to the need for a confederated Israel/Palestine, which would entail combining a vertical geopolitical partition with a horizontal power-sharing partition. The entire country would have to be cantonized on the basis of ethnic homogeneity, with broad powers granted to each ethnic canton. Statewide cultural and religious autonomy, power-sharing in the central government, a minority bill of rights, and special status for Jerusalem would create a binational state, the Confederation of Israel/Palestine.

Turning Israel/Palestine into a binational state is unacceptable to both sides. The Israelis believe "it amounts to the end of their state as the state of the Jewish people," and the Palestinians think it "turns their national problem into a question of civil and minority rights." In this phase of the process of reconciliation, there is no chance of such an idea becoming the focus of concrete political discourse. The experience of countries that have tried to create multi-ethnic systems in a single geopolitical entity is far from encouraging. There is no reason to believe that an ethnic confederation will succeed in Israel/Palestine, when such entities have failed or been destroyed by ethnic civil wars in Lebanon, Cyprus, Yugoslavia, and Sri Lanka, among other countries. But one might also point to Belgium or Canada, where strong forces militating for separation are checked by an overriding need to preserve economic and political cooperation.

The political and ideological resistance to the idea of a confederated Israel/Palestine is thus enormous, and the chances of its success are slim. However, raising the idea is important, for it challenges the traditional stereotypes—those that turned geopolitical structures into unquestionable precepts of belief. Israeli Jews support political and physical separation from "the Arabs" because they wish to detach themselves from an alien civilization and attach themselves to the "Western World." For them, the sea separating them from Europe is a geographical aberration, and they behave as though they were living somewhere between Paris and Prague.

Many Palestinians believe that this is where Israeli Jews should actually live. But there are both Israeli Jews and Palestinians who dream of Israel/Palestine, undivided in its physical and human landscapes, pluralistic and open; a country in which cultural relations, human interaction, intimate coexistence, and attachment to a common homeland will be stronger than militant tribalism and segregation in national ghettos. Those dreamers are entitled to suggest a system that combines ethnic and cultural separation within a common geopolitical framework on the basis of national equality and a clear definition of the rights and obligations of the two ethnic components coexisting in it. Israeli-Palestinian reconciliation is still a dream. There is a place for that dream too.

NOTES ON SOURCES

CHAPTER ONE

Quotations from the commissions of inquiry on the Temple Mount massacre were taken from the official documents and from Israeli Hebrew newspapers and were translated by the author. Information and analysis on Jerusalem are based on a lifelong involvement in Jerusalem's affairs as both an observer and a participant. The author's published works on the subject include *Jerusalem: The Torn City* (Minneapolis: University of Minnesota Press, 1977); *Jerusalem: Study of a Polarized Community* (Jerusalem: West Bank Database Project, 1984); *The Jerusalem Question: Problems, Procedures, and Options* (Jerusalem: West Bank Database Project, 1985). Interviews and newspaper clippings are in the author's archives.

CHAPTER TWO

Information and analysis on the West Bank settlements are based on research conducted by the West Bank Database Project (1982–90) and directed by the author.

CHAPTER THREE

Information and analysis on the Intifada and on Israeli Arabs are based on the computerized Israeli and Palestinian newspaper clippings compiled by the West Bank Database Project, on interviews, and on the author's columns in *Ha'aretz*, an Israeli Hebrew newspaper.

CHAPTERS FOUR, FIVE, AND SIX

These chapters are based on research and documentation compiled for the author's column in *Ha'aretz* and for the Hebrew-language book *Mekhol ha'kharadot* (Jerusalem: Keter, 1992). All quotations without sources are in the author's files, which include audio cassettes.

All quotations from Hebrew works have been translated by the author.

INDEX